California Bar Examination

Essay Questions and Selected Answers

February 2016

The State Bar Of California
Committee of Bar Examiners/Office of Admissions

180 Howard Street • San Francisco, CA 94105-1639 • (415) 538-2300
845 S. Figueroa Street • Los Angeles, CA 90017-2515 • (213) 765-1500

ESSAY QUESTIONS AND SELECTED ANSWERS

FEBRUARY 2016

CALIFORNIA BAR EXAMINATION

This publication contains the six essay questions from the February 2016 California Bar Examination and two selected answers for each question.

The answers were assigned high grades and were written by applicants who passed the examination after one read. The answers were produced as submitted by the applicant, except that minor corrections in spelling and punctuation were made for ease in reading. They are reproduced here with the consent of the authors.

Question Number	Subject
1.	Trusts
2.	Torts
3.	Professional Responsibility
4.	Remedies
5.	Evidence
6.	Contracts

ESSAY EXAMINATION INSTRUCTIONS

Your answer should demonstrate your ability to analyze the facts in the question, to tell the difference between material facts and immaterial facts, and to discern the points of law and fact upon which the case turns. Your answer should show that you know and understand the pertinent principles and theories of law, their qualifications and limitations, and their relationships to each other.

Your answer should evidence your ability to apply the law to the given facts and to reason in a logical, lawyer-like manner from the premises you adopt to a sound conclusion. Do not merely show that you remember legal principles. Instead, try to demonstrate your proficiency in using and applying them.

If your answer contains only a statement of your conclusions, you will receive little credit. State fully the reasons that support your conclusions, and discuss all points thoroughly.

Your answer should be complete, but you should not volunteer information or discuss legal doctrines that are not pertinent to the solution of the problem.

Unless a question expressly asks you to use California law, you should answer according to legal theories and principles of general application.

QUESTION 1

Wendy, a widow, owned a house in the city and a ranch in the country. She created a valid inter vivos trust, naming herself and her daughter, Dot, as co-trustees, and providing that she had the power to revoke or amend the trust at any time in writing, by a document signed by her and delivered to her and Dot as co-trustees. At Wendy's death, Dot was to become the sole trustee, and was directed to hold the assets in trust for the benefit of Wendy's sister, Sis, until Sis's death. At Sis's death, the trust was to terminate and all assets be distributed to Dot. The sole asset in the trust was Wendy's ranch.

Years later, Wendy prepared a valid will in which she stated, "I hereby revoke the trust I previously established, and leave my house and my ranch to my son, Sam, as trustee, to be held in trust for the benefit of my brother, Bob. Five years after my death the trust shall terminate, and all assets then remaining in the trust shall be distributed outright to Sam."

Wendy died. Following her death, both Dot and Sam were surprised to find her will.

Dot has refused to serve as trustee under the inter vivos trust, and claims that, as a result, the trust fails and that the ranch should immediately be given to her.

Sam has agreed to serve as trustee under the testamentary trust, and claims that the ranch is part of the trust. Sam then sells the house, at fair market price, to himself in his individual capacity, and invests all the assets of the trust into his new business, Sam's Solar. Bob objects to sale of the house and to Sam's investment.

1. What interests, if any, do Dot, Sam, and/or Bob have in the house and the ranch? Discuss.

2. What duties, if any, has Sam violated as trustee of the testamentary trust, and what remedies, if any, does Bob have against him? Discuss.

QUESTION 1: SELECTED ANSWER A

1. What interests held?

Dot

Valid trust

A valid trust is created when a settlor has the intent to give property (res) to the beneficiary in a bifurcated transfer. The settlor gives the res to the trustee, who has legal title, to hold for the benefit of the beneficiary, who holds equitable title. The trust need not be in writing unless required to by the statute of frauds, for example transferring an interest in land. The beneficiary need be ascertained but the trustee does not have to be. The trust can be revocable or irrevocable and it is presumed irrevocable unless otherwise stated.

Here, Wendy created a trust which had an ascertained beneficiary, her sister, and named herself and her daughter, Dot, as trustees. The res is the ranch. She further explicitly stated in the trust that it is revocable. The facts further state that the trust is a valid inter vivos trust.

Revocation/Termination of trust

A trust can be revoked if the settlor is alive and has explicitly reserved the right to revoke the trust. Otherwise it can only be terminated if the material purposes of the trust have been fulfilled.

Here, Wendy explicitly reserved the right to revoke the trust. She further explicitly stated the way in which the trust must be revoked. She stated that the trust can be revoked or amended "at any time in writing, by a document signed by her and delivered to her and Dot as co-trustees." Wendy later executed a valid will explicitly revoking the trust. This satisfies the writing requirement. It can be assumed that the will was "delivered" to Wendy because it was found at her death. However, the will was not delivered to Dot. Dot and Sam were both surprised to find the will at Wendy's death and it seems were surprised by its contents as well. It seems Wendy never gave Dot any other writing indicating the revocation of the trust or informed her verbally. Since Dot was not delivered a writing revoking the trust, and since that was one of the explicit conditions upon which the trust could be revoked, the trust was not properly revoked by the will. Therefore, the trust is still valid and still contains the ranch property.

Appointing a Trustee

A trust will fail if it does not have an ascertained beneficiary or if it does not have any property currently in it, except for a pour-over trust. However, the trust will not fail if a trustee has not been named or if a trustee either refuses to serve or needs to be removed by the beneficiaries or the Court. The Court will appoint a trustee, or the beneficiaries may vote on a trustee.

Here, Dot claims that she will refuse to serve as trustee and as a result the trust will fail. This is not the case. Instead, the court will appoint a trustee to hold the res for the benefit of Sis. Alternatively, Sis may argue that she should be allowed to vote for who will be appointed trustee and the court may allow that as an alternative. Either way the trust will not fail.

Remainder Interest

A remainder is a future interest that vests upon the termination of a life estate. It is vested if the beneficiary is ascertained and there are no conditions precedent.

Here, the trust states that the res is to be used for the benefit of Sis until her death. Upon the death of Sis all assets will be distributed to Dot. Dot is ascertained and there are no conditions precedent to her taking; she will take immediately upon the death of

Sis. Therefore, Dot has a vested remainder interest in the trust property. Dot will receive the trust property upon the death of Sis, but not before. Therefore, Dot does not have any present possessory interest in the trust property but does have a future interest as a remainder.

Sam

Valid Will

A formal valid will is created when there is a writing that is signed by the testator and indicates present testamentary intent (intended this document to be her will) and is witnessed by two witnesses who sign the document as well.

Here there are no facts as to whether or not witnesses signed but the facts do say that Wendy prepared a valid will, therefore it can be assumed. Further it was in writing and establishes present testamentary intent as it contemplates her death.

Pour-Over Trust

A trust can be created by the language of the will. Therefore, the property is held in trust upon the death of the testator instead of being distributed through probate.

Here, Wendy created a pour-over trust when, in her will, she wrote that she leaves her house and her ranch to her son Sam "as trustee, to be held for the benefit of my brother, Bob." The will further states that five years after her death the trust shall terminate and the remaining assets will be distributed to Sam.

Specific Devise/ Res of the pour-over trust

A specific devise is a devise of property that can be distinguished from the other assets of the estate.

Here, Wendy left her house to Sam as trustee to be held for the benefit of Bob. Although Wendy also indicated that she wished to leave her ranch as well, the will did not properly revoke the prior trust (see argument above), so the ranch is not included in the current pour-over trust.

Shifting Executory Interest

An executory interest is a future interest that will divest (cut off) a prior interest upon the happening of a stated event. A shifting executory interest is one that divests a prior grantee.

Here, Sam's interest will divest Bob's interest (a prior grantee) upon the happening of a stated event (five years after Wendy's death). Therefore, Sam has a valid future interest in the house.

Bob

Present possessory Interest subject to an executory interest

A present possessory interest is when a person has a current interest in property. It is subject to an executory interest if it can be divested by a third party.

Here, Bob has a present possessory interest in the trust property. He does not have legal title over it because that is held by the trustee, but he has the right to receive the benefits of the trust as the beneficiary. He has this right until five years after Wendy's death when it will be cut off by Sam's interest. Therefore, it is subject to an executory interest.

2. What duties violated and what remedies available?

Duty of Loyalty

A trustee as a fiduciary has the duty of loyalty to the trust. He has the duty to act in a reasonable manner to ensure the best interests of the trust beneficiaries. He can violate this duty by self-dealing with the trust or by taking an action that would be adverse to the trust beneficiaries.

Here, Sam has engaged in self-dealing of the trust property. He has sold the house to himself in his individual capacity. Although he sold it at fair market price, this is still a breach of the duty of loyalty. It is never considered reasonable for a trustee to engage in self-dealing, unless the trust specifically states that he can do so and it still must be fair to the beneficiaries. Here the power to engage in self-dealing was not explicitly given to him in the trust. He further engaged in self-dealing by investing the assets of the trust into his own business. By selling the house to himself and by investing the assets in his own business, Sam has breached the duty of loyalty.

Duty of Care

A trustee also has the duty to act as a reasonable person would in caring for the trust. He has the duty to use any special skills he may have and to treat the trust property as his own in his care for it.

Here the duty of care was broken because it is not reasonable for a trustee to sell assets of the trust to himself. It is further unreasonable to invest all the assets of the trust property in a single business.

Duty to Invest

At common law a trustee was limited to a specified list of investments that he was approved to make. Now trustees are expected to diversify investments in order to spread the risk of loss and the whole portfolio will be considered.

Here, Sam did not diversify the investments. He invested all the trust assets into a single business. This does not spread the risk of loss. If the business fails, the trust will lose all of its assets. Sam has breached this duty.

Duty of impartiality

The trustee has the duty to fairly balance the trust assets so that the current beneficiaries and remainder beneficiaries are treated fairly. The current beneficiary is entitled to the income and the future beneficiary is entitled to the principal. The trustee must make sure to balance the income and principal when making his investments so that one does not increase drastically while the other depreciates.

Here Sam has not been impartial. He has sold the trust property to himself and invested all of it in his own business. This may yield high income or it may not. Even if this will benefit Bob more than it will benefit him, he still had the duty to be impartial when making his investments so that neither the income nor the principal drastically decreases. He has breached this duty.

Duty to inform beneficiaries

The trustee also has the duty to keep beneficiaries reasonably informed about major decisions including the trust property.

Bob knows and objects to the sale of the house and the investment. It is unclear whether Sam told him about this before taking the actions. If he did not, he has breached his duty to keep the beneficiary informed.

Removal as trustee

A trustee who breaches his duties may be removed as a trustee. A trustee can also be removed for other reasons such as death or incapacity or if a serious conflict exists with the beneficiary.

Here, Sam has breached a number of his duties as discussed above. Therefore, Bob may seek to have him removed as a trustee and the court will likely approve it.

Monetary damages

A beneficiary is entitled to seek monetary damages from a trustee who has breached his duty. He can seek damages that the trust would have been entitled to absent the breach. He may be able to instead get unjust enrichment damages from the trustee.

Here, Bob can likely get either the profits that Sam received from the sale or of the house and the investment in the business or he can receive the full value of the house back.

QUESTION 1: SELECTED ANSWER B

I. What Interests if any, do Dot, Sam, and/or Bob have in the house and the ranch?

First Inter Vivos Trust

An inter vivos trust is created during the life of the grantor. There are two types: private express trusts and charitable trusts. There must be some indication that the grantor intends to part with the property if the grantor is the sole beneficiary. Here, the facts indicate that Wendy created a valid inter vivos trust.

Private Express Trust

A private express trust is where the grantor creates a trust for the benefit of one or more ascertainable beneficiaries. It must comply with the valid trust requirements.
Here, Wendy created a trust during her lifetime. The beneficiaries are Sis and Dot. Thus, because Sis and Dot are ascertainable beneficiaries, this is a private express trust. It must comport with the trust requirements.

Valid Trust

A valid trust requires (i) a grantor, (ii) intent to create a trust, (iii) ascertainable beneficiaries, (iv) a trustee, (v) trust property, or res, and (vi) a valid trust purpose.

Grantor
The grantor is the person who creates the trust.
Here, Wendy is the person who created the trust and is thus the grantor.

Intent to Create a Trust
The grantor must intend to create the trust.

Here, the facts indicate that Wendy created a valid inter vivos trust.

Thus, there is intent to create a trust.

Ascertainable Beneficiaries

The trust must have ascertainable beneficiaries to whom the trust property can be transferred to.

Here, Sis and Dot are the beneficiaries.

Thus, there are ascertainable beneficiaries.

Trustee

A trust must have a trustee although a lack of one at creation does not create an invalid trust. Instead, the court will appoint a trustee.

Here, Wendy and Dot are co-trustees.

Thus, the trust has trustees.

Trust Property

A trust must have trust property. This can be tangible or intangible assets and can include land property.

Here, the trust property is Wendy's ranch.

Thus, the trust is properly funded.

Trust Purpose

A trust must be created for a valid trust purpose. Generally, any purpose is valid as long as it is not illegal.

Here, the trust is created for the benefit of Sis and Dot.

Thus, there is a valid trust purpose.

Revocation of Trust by Will

Generally, a trust is presumed to be irrevocable unless the grantor expressly reserves the right to modify or terminate the trust.

Here, Wendy expressly reserved her right to revoke or amend the trust at any time in writing, provided that the document be signed by her and delivered to her and Dot as trustees. Wendy did in fact attempt to revoke the trust when she prepared a valid will stating that she revokes the trust previously established.

Dot has two arguments that the trust has not been revoked. First, as a co-trustee, she will argue that there needed to be unanimous agreement between her and Wendy in order to revoke the trust. This argument would fail though because the grantor is the one who gets to reserve the right to revoke. This does not depend on whether or not the grantor is also a trustee. Thus, Wendy could have acted on her own.

Dot's second argument would be that Wendy did not follow the instructions for revoking the trust. The trust states that a signed document needed to be delivered to Wendy and Dot as co-trustees. However, Dot was surprised to find the will when Wendy died.

Thus, it is debatable whether or not the trust was properly revoked. If the court chooses to strictly read the instructions provided for in the original trust, then it might find that the trust was never revoked because Wendy failed to deliver the signed document to both Wendy and Dot. Therefore, the trust would still be valid and Dot would be entitled to the ranch once Sis died, as provided for in the trust.

Trustee Termination

As mentioned before, a trust does not terminate because there is no trustee. If a trustee has not been named, or a trustee does not wish to serve as trustee, then the court will designate a trustee.

Here, the facts indicate that Dot does not want to serve as trustee. Therefore, the court will appoint one instead.

Thus, Dot's argument that the trust fails and she should be given the ranch is incorrect. Instead, a trustee will be appointed to carry out the trust duties. The ranch will be held in trust for the benefit of Sis until her death. At that time, Dot will receive the ranch.

Testamentary Trust

A testamentary trust is one that is created in the grantor's will. It must comply with all wills requirements in the state where the will is executed.

Here, the facts indicate that Dot executed a valid will creating a new trust. As mentioned before, the trust must also comply with specific requirements.

Trust Requirements

A valid trust requires (i) a grantor, (ii) intent to create a trust, (iii) ascertainable beneficiaries, (iv) a valid trust purpose, (v) trust property, and (vi) a trustee.

Here, Wendy is the creator of the trust and she intended to do so as stated in her will. Bob is a valid ascertainable beneficiary. Keeping the trust for Bob and Sam's benefits are valid trust purposes. There is trust property, although as mentioned before the ranch is likely not going to be held in this trust because Wendy failed to properly revoke her earlier trust. However, even without the ranch, the house is still included in the trust property and satisfies the trust res requirement. Finally, there is a trustee - Sam.

Thus, Wendy has created a valid testamentary trust but it will only hold the house as trust property.

Disposition:

Ranch:

The ranch is still held in the first trust because the first trust was not validly revoked. A new trustee will be appointed and it will be held in trust for the benefit of Sis for her life. Upon Sis' death, Dot will receive the remaining assets of the ranch.

House:

The house should be held in trust for Bob and in five years, the house will go to Sam.

II. What Duties, if any, has Sam violated as trustee of the testamentary trust, and what remedies, if any, does Bob have against him?

Trustee Duties

A trustee is tasked with safeguarding the trust assets and holding them for the benefit of the beneficiaries. He must distribute the trust assets in accordance with the trust terms. He owes the beneficiaries duties of loyalty and care.

A trustee is tasked with safeguarding the trust assets and holding them for the benefit of the beneficiaries. He owes the beneficiaries a duty of loyalty and care. He must distribute the trust assets in accordance with the trust. Traditionally, there was an enumerated list of statutory duties a trustee owed to the trust. Today, the standard is more along the lines of acting as a reasonably prudent person would.

Duty of Loyalty

A trustee owes a duty of loyalty to the trust. This can be broken when the trustee puts his interests before the trust's. Specifically, this can be broken through self-dealing.

Self-Dealing

A trustee can breach the duty of loyalty through self-dealing. This occurs when the trustee interacts and benefits with the trust assets for his own benefit. Self-dealing is a per se breach of the duty of loyalty. Once self-dealing has been proven, there are no further questions asked. It does not matter that the self-dealing was beneficial for the trust or at the fair market price. Furthermore, even if the trust allows for self-dealing, it must be reasonable.

House:

Here, Sam is the trustee of Wendy's second trust. He has sold the house to himself at fair market value. This is per se self-dealing. As mentioned before, it is not a defense that Sam sold the house at a fair market value.

Trust Assets:

In addition to selling himself the house, he also invested all assets of the trust into his new business. This is another instance of per se self-dealing.

Thus, Sam breached his duty of loyalty.

Duty of Care

A trustee must act as a reasonably prudent person would. He must reasonably believe in good faith that his actions are for the benefit of the trust. A trustee has the normal powers to sell, buy, and invest trust property as a reasonably prudent person would. This includes duties of prudence and duties of impartiality.

Duty of Prudence

A trustee must act as a reasonably prudent person would under the circumstances. If the trustee has any special skills, then he is held to the standard of that skilled person. This duty extends to investments of the trust property.

Here, Sam sold the entire house - which constitutes the entire trust property, thus ending the trust. A reasonably prudent person would not do this especially since the reasonably prudent person is tasked with managing the trust property for the benefit of the life beneficiaries and the remaindermen. Sam might argue that the house was going to go to him in five years anyways, but this disregards the duties he owes to Bob during the current five years. Sam might also argue that he believed the ranch was in the trust and thus the trust would still properly be funded. This argument will also likely fail because Sam and Wendy both knew about the will and likely knew that the ranch was contested. If Sam truly believed that the ranch was part of his trust, he should have at least waited until that was concretely determined.

Thus, because Sam sold all of the trust property, and did not act as a reasonable prudent person, he breached his duty of prudence.

Duty of Impartiality

Traditionally, in a trust, the principal went to the remaindermen and the income went to the life beneficiaries. Modernly, the trustee is instead to balance the interests of the remaindermen and the principal equally instead of favoring one over the other.

Here, Sam sold the entire house; this is not only a breach of the duty of prudence, as mentioned before, but also a breach of duty to be impartial. As mentioned previously, nothing remains now for Bob. The interests of the life beneficiary have not been taken into account.

Thus, Sam has breached his duty of being impartial.

Remedies

Constructive Trust

A constructive trust can be imposed on the person holding the trust property if they improperly received the trust property, there is inadequate legal remedy, and the person currently holding the property would be unjustly enriched.

Here, as described above, Sam improperly holds the trust property because he received it by breaching his duty of loyalty and duty of prudence. Furthermore, because the property is a house, it is considered unique and thus there are inadequate legal remedies. Finally, Sam would be unjustly enriched because he would be allowed to keep the house and he is doing so for five years more than he should have.

Thus, the court can impose a constructive trust on the house for Bob's benefit.

Trustee Removal

When a trustee has breached his duties, the beneficiaries can seek to remove the trustee.

Here, as described above, Sam violated trustee duties - particularly that of the duty of prudence and the duty of loyalty.

Thus, the court should remove Sam as a trustee and should appoint a different trustee should the trust continue.

Tracing

Finally, when there is self-dealing and assets are invested, the beneficiaries can seek to retrieve the funds through tracing.

Here, Sam invested the trust assets in his new business.

Thus, Bob can seek to trace these funds and retrieve them for the benefit of the trust.

QUESTION 2

Jack believed that extraterrestrial aliens had come to earth, were living undercover as humans, and were planning a full-scale invasion in the future. Jack believed that his next-door neighbor, Nancy, was one of these aliens.

One day, Nancy called Jack on the phone to complain that Jack's children were playing in her yard. Jack yelled that his children could play wherever they wanted to. He also said that he was going to kill her.

The next day, Nancy approached Jack, who was playing in his yard with his children. She reminded him to keep his children out of her yard. Jack picked up a chainsaw and said, "When the invasion comes, I am going to use this baby to cut off your head!"

From the other side of the street, Ben saw Jack angrily raise the chainsaw at Nancy. Ben ran across the street and knocked Jack to the ground and injured him.

Later that week, Jack decided that he could wait no longer. He saw Nancy's car, which he believed to be an alien spaceship, parked on the street. He snuck over to her car and cut the brake lines, hoping Nancy would have a minor accident and be taught a lesson.

Unaware that her car had been tampered with, Nancy lent it to Paul. When the brakes failed to work, Paul drove off a mountain road and was severely injured.

1. What tort causes of action, if any, may Nancy bring against Jack, and how is each likely to fare? Discuss.

2. What tort causes of action, if any, may Jack bring against Ben, and how is each likely to fare? Discuss.

3. What tort causes of action, if any, may Paul bring against Jack, and how is each likely to fare? Discuss.

QUESTION 2: SELECTED ANSWER A

Whether Jack can be held liable for Intentional Torts

As a preliminary matter, the overarching issue is whether Jack can be found guilty of intentional torts, where he believed that extraterrestrial aliens had come to earth, were living undercover as humans, and were planning a full-scale invasion in the future. Jack further believed that his next-door neighbor, Nancy, was one of these aliens. Jack will argue that, because of his delusions, he does not have the requisite intent necessary to be liable for an intentional tort. Nancy will argue that, so long as Jack intended his actions, it does not matter that the action was motivated by a delusion. A court is likely to find that Jack can be found liable for intentional torts, as he had both the intent to act and the intent to achieve certain results from those actions. The fact that the actions were motivated by an insane delusion will not be a valid defense to the intentional tort actions that may be brought by Nancy and Paul.

Nancy's Tort Causes of Action Against Jack

Assault

At issue is whether Jack assaulted Nancy when he threatened to kill her when they were talking on the phone, and/or when he raised the chainsaw up while they were talking in the yard.

Assault is the intentional creation of apprehension in another of immediate bodily harm. "Apprehension" means that the victim must be aware of the threat against her. Assault requires more than just threatening words alone - the words must be accompanied by an action. Conversely, words may negate immediacy by attaching a condition or time frame to a threat. Here, Nancy could argue that Jack assaulted her twice - once when he said that he was going to kill her when they were talking on the phone, and once when he threatened her with a chainsaw when they were on the lawn.

As to the phone conversation, Jack yelled that he was going to kill Nancy while they were talking on the phone. Nancy will likely not succeed on this claim of assault because the conversation took place over the phone, and, thus, was not accompanied with a threatening action (that Nancy could see, at any rate) that would cause Nancy to believe that she was in danger or immediate bodily harm. Because she and Jack were in separate houses during the phone call, Nancy would likely not be able to demonstrate that she was in apprehension of *immediate* bodily harm. Thus, this cause of action for assault would fail.

Nancy's cause of action for assault relating to the chainsaw incident is stronger, although it is still likely to fail. After Nancy approached Jack outdoors, reminding him to keep his children off her lawn, Jack raised a chainsaw and said "When the invasion comes, I am going to use this baby to cut off your head!" Raising the chainsaw definitely qualifies as an action that would accompany the threatening words to create an apprehension of immediate bodily harm in Nancy. Additionally, the threat of cutting off Nancy's head would cause apprehension. Jack will argue, however, that his words negated the immediacy required for an assault cause of action, because he stated that he would cut off Nancy's head "when the invasion comes." These words attached a future time condition to the threat, thereby negating the immediacy. Nancy could argue, on the other hand, that since the "invasion" was a delusion by Jack, the time frame could be immediate, not future, as it is possible that, in Jack's mind, the invasion was going to happen right away. If Nancy's point of view prevailed, Jack would be liable for assault. However, since Jack was not screaming that the invasion had arrived, but rather was speaking of the invasion as if it were a future event, a court will likely find that his words negated immediacy, and despite the threatening action he is not liable for assault.

Intentional Infliction of Emotional Distress

The next issue is whether Jack's threats to kill Nancy, and to cut her head off with the chainsaw made to her face, make him liable for intentional infliction of emotional distress, even where she does not appear to have suffered any distress.

Nancy could raise a claim of intentional infliction of emotional distress, which requires for a defendant to commit outrageous conduct that causes severe distress in a plaintiff. Here, Jack's conduct was certainly outrageous, that is, it was outside the bounds of decency as upheld in society. By threatening to kill Nancy and threatening to cut off her head with a chainsaw, Jack clearly made outrageous statements that exceed the bounds of decency. However, there is no indication from the facts that Nancy was emotionally distressed as a result of Jack's statements. Although IIED does not require a showing of physical distress symptoms, there must be at least some allegation that the plaintiff suffered from severe distress. Absent that allegation, as here, there is not sufficient grounds for an IIED cause of action.

Battery

The next issue is whether Jack's tampering with Nancy's car results in a battery against Nancy.

Battery is the intentional infliction of bodily harm caused by harmful or offensive touching to another's person. Here, Jack intended to cause Nancy bodily harm - he was hoping that she would "have a minor accident" to be "taught a lesson." This indicates that, even if he only wished minor harm upon Nancy, Jack intended to cause Nancy bodily harm. Less clear is whether Jack's tampering with Nancy's car resulted in a "harmful or offensive touching to her person." A "person" may be construed liberally to include objects connected to a plaintiff's body, such as her purse. Nancy's car, however, when it was parked on the street, was not connected to her body and it is unlikely that a court would construe the car to be an extension of Nancy's person.

Nancy would argue, however, that battery need not be immediate, and that by cutting the brake lines Jack intended future harm to Nancy's person. Nancy would argue that Jack's actions were akin to poisoning someone - which is a battery even though the harm to a plaintiff's body does not occur until the future. Nancy would likely be successful on this argument if she had actually been injured by Jack's actions. Since

Paul was injured instead, the doctrine of transferred intent may apply (see below), but Nancy did not actually suffer a harm or offense to her person, and, ultimately, she will not be successful in her battery cause of action.

Trespass to Land

Trespass to land occurs when the Defendant unlawfully enters the land of the Plaintiff. Here, Jack cut the brake lines on Nancy's car while it was on the street, and there is nothing to indicate that he trespassed onto her land. Thus, Nancy does not have a claim for trespass to land.

Trespass to Chattel and Conversion

Trespass to chattel and conversion are property torts that occur when the Defendant damages or steals the property of a plaintiff. The difference between trespass to chattel and conversion is one of degree - trespass to chattel occurs where property is harmed but not completely destroyed, and conversion occurs when the property is destroyed or stolen. Here, Jack could be liable for both torts. He intentionally cut Nancy's car's brake lines, and, in so doing, could be liable for trespass to chattel, which means he would owe Nancy the cost of repair for the break lines. Subsequently, however, when Paul drove the car, he drove off a mountain road. These facts indicate that the car was destroyed. If that is the case, Jack could be liable for conversion, which means he would owe Nancy the market value of the car at the time the conversion occurred.

Jack's Tort Claims Against Ben

At issue is whether Jack may bring a claim of battery against Ben, where Ben knocked Jack to the ground and injured him after Ben saw Jack "angrily raise the chainsaw at Nancy." As discussed above, battery occurs when a defendant commits harmful or offensive touching to another's person. Here, Ben did harmfully touch Jack -

he "knocked Jack to the ground" and injured Jack, thereby meeting the requirements for a prima facie case of battery.

The next issue becomes whether Ben may raise any defenses against the battery cause of action. Ben may raise the defense of "defense of others" to protect him from liability for any battery committed against Jack. A person may use reasonable force in defense of another when that person believes that the other is in danger of immediate bodily harm. The force used must be proportionate to the threat. Here, it appears that Ben knocked Jack over in order to protect Nancy, whom he reasonably believed was in danger of being attacked by Jack with his chainsaw. Ben used reasonable, non-deadly force to defend Nancy (even though it could be argued that Jack's chainsaw was a deadly weapon). Ben did not escalate the force, but rather responded proportionately. Thus, Ben is likely to be found not liable for battery, because his defense of protection of others would be valid.

It should be noted that, even if Ben was mistaken about his need to defend Nancy, because Jack did not actually intend to harm Nancy until "the invasion comes", this mistake will not negate Ben's defense. Mistaken self-defense (or defense of others) is still a valid defense to an intentional tort so long as the mistake was reasonable. Here, it was reasonable for Ben - who was standing across the street and likely could not hear what Jack was saying - to believe that Nancy was in danger when Jack raised his chainsaw in an "angry" manner.

Paul's Tort Claims Against Jack

At issue is whether Paul may bring a battery cause of action against Jack, where Jack tampered with Nancy's car, which Paul then borrowed. Specifically, the issue is whether, because of the doctrine of transfer of intent, Jack's intention to harm Nancy could be transferred to Paul. Under the doctrine of transferred intent, the intent to commit an intentional tort, such as battery, against one plaintiff may be transferred to another plaintiff if the harm actually befalls the second plaintiff. As noted above, it is unlikely that a court will find that Jack committed battery against Nancy, because Nancy was not actually harmed or touched by Jack's actions. Paul, however, was "severely injured" as a result of Jack's attempt to commit a battery against Nancy. As a result, Paul may sue Jack under a theory of transferred intent, and Paul will likely be successful.

1. Nancy's Tort Claims Against Jack

A. Assault for Threat over Telephone

Nancy may bring an assault claim against Jack for the threat to kill her that he made over the phone, but this claim will not succeed.

To establish a prima facie case of assault, the plaintiff must show: (i) an act by the defendant that brings about a reasonable apprehension in the plaintiff of an immediate harmful or offensive contact to the plaintiff's person; (ii) intent by the defendant to cause such apprehension; and (iii) causation.

The facts show that while speaking over the phone, Jack told Nancy that he was going to kill her. A threat to kill someone is generally enough to create a reasonable apprehension in that person that they will suffer a harmful contact.

For the element of intent under most intentional torts, the defendant need not actually intend the specific result, but rather just be substantially certain that such result is likely to arise as a result of the act (general intent). Jack's intent to cause such apprehension can be shown by the fact that he can be substantially certain a threat to kill someone would cause them to fear a harmful contact. And causation may be shown because Jack's threat was what caused the apprehension of an immediate harmful contact.

However, Nancy's claim for assault will fail because the intentional tort of assault requires that the apprehension, or fear, be of an immediate harm. A threat of future harm is not sufficient for the tort of assault. Moreover, the reasonable apprehension may not be created by words alone--there must be some threatening act in addition to the words.

Here, Nancy was speaking to Jack over the phone, and thus was not in his presence when he made the threat. Therefore, her apprehension could not have been of an immediate harm, because he was not present to execute on his threat. He would have had to run next door to make good on his threat to kill her (at which point the threat would have been immediate, but not until then).

B. Assault with Chainsaw

Nancy may also bring an assault claim for Jack's threat with the chainsaw. Here, Jack's conduct amounted to more than a mere threat, as he was brandishing a chainsaw. The combination of telling Nancy he would cut off Nancy's head while lifting a chainsaw is certainly enough to cause a reasonable person to fear that she will suffer a harmful contact--here, in the form of a chainsaw to the head.

Nancy will argue that the immediacy requirement is fulfilled because Jack is standing right next to Nancy, and thus can cause the harm at that moment. However, Nancy is likely to lose on this claim as well, because the existence of conditional words will neutralize the immediacy of the threat. Jack told Nancy he will cut her head off "when the invasion comes." Nancy probably has no idea what he is talking about and when that invasion will supposedly arrive, but from Jack's words it seems clear that the invasion will come in the future. Since he is threatening to cut off her head in the future, there is no reasonable apprehension of an immediate contact to Nancy's person, and thus no assault.

C. Intentional Infliction of Emotional Distress (IIED)

Nancy can bring IIED claims for both Jack's threat over the phone and the threat while picking up the chainsaw, so long as she is able to show that she suffered severe emotional distress as a result of such threats.

To establish a prima facie case of IIED, the plaintiff must show: (i) an act by the defendant amounting to extreme and outrageous conduct; (ii) intent by the defendant to cause the plaintiff severe emotional distress; (iii) causation; and (iv) the plaintiff suffered damages in the form of severe emotional distress.

Both the threat over the phone call and the threat in the yard amount to extreme and outrageous conduct, because both involve threats to kill Nancy. A threat to kill someone is definitely extreme and outrageous, and would shock the sensibilities of an ordinary, reasonable person.

The intent element for IIED requires that the defendant intend to cause severe emotional distress, or recklessness as to such a result. Here, the required consent will be found via recklessness--Jack's threat to kill Nancy is a complete disregard of a substantial risk that such a threat will cause his neighbor to fear for her life and safety, and thus suffer severe emotional distress.

Nancy's only potential pitfall on this claim is that there is nothing in the facts that show she suffered severe emotional distress. Such distress does not need to take the form of a physical manifestation, but she does need to show substantial distress (e.g. severe anxiety or fear for her life). Assuming she is able to show such distress, Nancy will prevail on an IIED claim against Jack.

D. Conversion/Trespass to Chattels

Nancy can also bring a claim for conversion for Jack's act of cutting the brakes on her car.

To establish a prima facie case of conversion, the plaintiff must show: (i) an act by the defendant that interferes with the plaintiff's right of possession in a chattel; (ii) intent by the defendant to so interfere; and (iii) causation.

The claim of trespass to chattels has the identical elements, the difference between the torts being in degree of the interference. Conversion requires that the interference with the plaintiff's possession interest be so substantial in quality or nature that it justifies forcing the defendant to pay the full fair market value of the chattel, whereas a more minor interference constitutes trespass to chattel (and Jack would need to pay only the amount of damage caused by the interference).

Here, Jack cut the brakes on Nancy's car, which led the next person driving the car to crash it and presumably damage it further. Thus causation is shown, and the facts show Jack intentionally cut the brakes. Because of the severe damage to her car, Nancy will be able to recover under conversion for its full value.

E. Trespass to Land

Finally, Nancy may bring an action against Jack for trespass since his kids were on her property. However, this action is unlikely to succeed, since a parent is not vicariously liable for the actions of his children. Nancy would need to bring this action against the children themselves.

2. Jack's Tort Claims Against Ben

A. Battery for Tackle

To establish a prima facie case of battery, the plaintiff must show: (i) an act by the defendant bringing about a harmful or offensive contact to the plaintiff's person; (ii) intent by the defendant to bring about such contact; and (iii) causation.

Here, Ben tackled Jack to the ground and injured him, which shows a harmful contact and causation. From the facts, it appears that Ben intended such a contact because he ran across the street and knocked Jack to the ground to protect Nancy.

Jack will have a strong argument against the battery via defense of others. Defense of others is a defense that will prevent Jack from succeeding on this claim. One has the right to defend another if the defendant reasonably believes that that person would be entitled to defend themselves. Here, Ben saw Jack raise the chainsaw and may have even heard him threaten to cut off her head. A reasonable person would believe that Nancy was in danger, and thus Ben acted reasonably by defending her. He used non-deadly force in confronting Jack's potentially deadly force, and thus the type of force he used was appropriate.

Thus Ben will not be liable for battery.

B. Trespass to Land

Jack may also bring a claim for trespass to land against Ben for running onto his property. To show this tort, the plaintiff must show that the defendant interfered with his possession of land; intent; and causation. By intentionally running onto his property, Jack will claim Ben committed this tort.

However, Ben will argue that he was justified in running on his property as a result of a public necessity. A public necessity creates an absolute privilege to enter the land of another. Here, the necessity was Nancy's potential decapitation. Thus Ben will not be liable for this tort.

3. Paul's Tort Actions Against Jack

A. Battery

Paul should bring an action against Jack for battery (see elements above). Paul will show that by cutting the brakes on the car, Jack was substantially certain that a harmful contact would arise in the person of the driver.

Transferred Intent

While Jack may argue that he only intended to harm Nancy, rather than Paul, the doctrine of transferred intent will provide the intent needed to find Jack liable for the tort of battery against Paul.

Under this doctrine, when a person intends to commit an intentional tort against another, but instead: a different tort results against that same person; the same tort arises against a different person; or a different tort arises against a different person; the tortfeasor's initial intent to commit the first tort will provide the requisite intent for the second tort. Transferred intent is available for the intentional tort of battery.

Here, Jack intended to cause a harmful contact to Nancy. The fact that Paul was the first to drive the car, rather than Nancy, will not relieve Jack of liability. Jack's intent to harm Paul will be found via the doctrine of transferred intent, and Jack will be liable for battery.

Defense of Insanity

Jack may argue he did not have the intent necessary to commit the tort because of his insanity, given his belief that the car was an alien spaceship. However, insanity is not a defense to an intentional tort unless the mental defect is such that the tortfeasor does not understand the nature of his act. Here, Jack was aware that he was cutting the brakes with intent to harm Nancy, and thus insanity will not be a valid defense.

QUESTION 3

Contractor and Lawyer had been in a consensual sexual relationship for months. Contractor could not afford to hire an experienced lawyer to defend him against Plaintiff's complex construction defect case and to bring a cross-complaint. Contractor told Lawyer, who had never handled such matters, that he wouldn't sue her for malpractice if she would defend him for half her regular rate. Lawyer felt pressured because of their relationship.

Lawyer told Contractor she would defend him for half-price, but she would only bring his cross-complaint on contingency at her regular rate of 30 percent of any recovery. Contractor agreed. Although they continued to have sexual relations, their personal relationship deteriorated. Lawyer forgot to make a scheduled court appearance in the case.

At trial Plaintiff lost, and Contractor won $100,000 on his cross-complaint. Lawyer deposited the $100,000 in her Client Trust Account. She told Contractor she would send him $70,000. Contractor said Lawyer must send an additional $15,000 because she agreed to represent him for half-price on everything, including the contingency fee.

1. Did Lawyer commit any ethical violation by agreeing to represent Contractor? Discuss.

2. Did Lawyer commit any ethical violation by failing to make the court appearance? Discuss.

3. What should Lawyer do with the money in the Client Trust Account? Discuss.

Answer according to California and ABA authorities.

QUESTION 3: SELECTED ANSWER A

1. L committed several ethical violations when she agreed to represent C:

The ABA Model Rules of Professional Conduct ("ABA Rules") and the California Rules of Professional Conduct ("CA Rules") both contain provisions relating to sexual relationships with clients. The ABA Rules prohibit sexual relationships with clients, unless there was a preexisting sexual relationship. The CA Rules also allow for a preexisting sexual relationship, but also allow for new sexual relationships so long as sex is not a condition for professional representation, the client is not unduly influenced or coerced into sex, and the lawyer's performance is not negatively affected by the sexual relationship. Here, Contractor ("C") and Lawyer ("L") had already been in a consensual sexual relationship for months prior to L agreeing to represent C. Therefore, this would not be an ethical violation under the ABA Rules by itself because the sexual relationship was already existing at the time L agreed to represent C. The relationship may be considered a violation under the CA Rules, because while it was a preexisting relationship, L's performance and representation of C deteriorated such that she forgot to make a court appearance in the case.

L may have also violated the duty of loyalty. When there is a significant risk that the interests of another client, the lawyer, or a third person could materially limit the representation of the client, there is a conflict of interest. Here, the lawyer's own personal interest in attempting to appease her lover could be seen as materially limiting her competent representation of C, as it would be difficult to separate their personal relationship from the professional one. Further, L felt pressured to take on the case, and it is arguably likely that her professional obligations could be also subject to pressure from C.

L also agreed to represent C despite not having any experience in complex construction defect cases. Under the ABA Rules, a lawyer has a duty of competence, which is to possess the necessary skill, knowledge, preparation and thoroughness reasonably necessary to represent the client. If the lawyer does not have the requisite competence, the lawyer must either learn the law without undue delay or expense, or associate with a lawyer who is well-versed in the law (subject to client approval in bringing on this new lawyer). Since L was not experienced in complex construction defect cases, and does not appear to have taken any action to educate herself in this field of practice or associate with a lawyer who is experienced in these matters, she breached her duty of competence. Further, she failed to appear at a scheduled court hearing, which is also a violation of her duty of competence that may subject her to disciplinary action. Under the CA Rules, a lawyer has breached her duty of competence if the lawyer intentionally, recklessly or repeatedly fails to provide competent representation would they be subject to discipline. Here, L may be found to have been in violation of the CA Rules as well since she intentionally or at least recklessly took on the matter while knowing she was not qualified to do so (and only took it on because she felt pressured). The failure to appear at court because she forgot may not rise to a violation of the CA Rules; however, since it does not appear to be intentional, reckless or repeated - it is probably negligent at the most.

L also agreed to represent C if he wouldn't sue her for malpractice if she would defend him for half her regular rate. Under the ABA Rules, a lawyer may not limit a client's right to seek disciplinary action or to participate in an investigation. The ABA Rules allow for the client and lawyer to limit malpractice liability, so long as the client is represented by independent counsel. The CA Rules, however, expressly forbid any limitation of malpractice liability. Therefore, L is in breach of the ABA Rules because C was not represented by an independent attorney when L's malpractice liability was limited, and is in breach of the CA Rules because they do not allow for any limitation on malpractice liability.

Further, L agreed to represent C for a contingency fee for the cross-complaint, but it does not appear the fee agreement was in writing. A contingency fee agreement under the ABA Rules must be in writing, state the percentage of fees that the lawyer would receive, what expenses would be deducted from recovery, and whether the lawyer's percentage would be deducted before or after expenses were deducted. Under the CA Rules, the fee agreement must also state how other costs will be paid, as well as that the fees are negotiable. Here, it does not appear that L and C entered into a fee agreement, but rather orally agreed on the contingency.

Note that the agreement to represent C for half price under the ABA Rules did not have to be in writing, but under the CA Rules likely should have been. The CA Rules require written agreements for non-contingency fees unless the fees will be under $1,000, is for a corporate client, is for routine matters, the client agrees otherwise in a separate writing, or there is an emergency or other good reason. Here, it is likely even with L's fees being half price for defending C, the fees will be over $1,000; the matter is not for a corporate client but is instead for C individually; the case is not a routine matter that L normally handles for C; C has not agreed otherwise in a separate writing; and there is no emergency or other good reason. Therefore, L would be in violation of the CA Rules because her agreement to defend C for half her normal price was not in writing.

2. L committed several ethical violations when she failed to make the court appearance:

As stated above, L owed C a duty of competence. She breached this duty under the ABA Rules by agreeing to take on his matter without experience, and also by failing to appear at court. She likely breached this duty under the CA Rules by intentionally agreeing to take on a matter in which she was not experienced, but would probably not be in breach under the CA Rules for failing to appear, as this did not appear to be intentional, reckless or repeated conduct on her part.

L also breached her duty of care. A lawyer must act in good faith and as a reasonably prudent person with the same care, skills and caution as would be expended on her own matters. L breached this duty by failing to appear at court, as a reasonably prudent person would not have forgotten to make a scheduled court appearance.

L also breached her duty of diligence to C. A lawyer has a duty to pursue cases to completion, and to diligently represent clients in their matters. Part of this duty under the ABA Rules is the duty to act promptly and expedite a client's case if it is in the client's best interest. Under the CA Rules, the lawyer may not unduly delay for improper purposes or for her own convenience. She breached the duty of diligence because she failed to appear. If she caused a delay in the proceedings due to the rescheduling of the court appearance, she again breached this duty.

3. L should send C the undisputed amount from the Client Trust Account, and is entitled to keep the disputed amount in the Client Trust Account until the dispute is settled.

A lawyer has the duty to notify the client and distribute client funds promptly when funds have been received on the client's behalf, and to distribute funds to third parties (if the client knows and has consented to having third parties being paid out of the client trust account). Here, it appears L has properly maintained a separate client trust account for C. When L deposited the $100,000 in the Client Trust Account, she also appeared to have promptly told C that the funds had arrived. However, C disputed the amount L was to send - L said she would send $70,000, which reflects the $100,000 minus her 30% contingency fee, but C said the contingency fee should also have been half price, so only 15%. Therefore, C claims L should send him $85,000. When there is a dispute as to the fees owed, the lawyer must send the undisputed portion to the client, and is entitled to keep the disputed portion in the client trust account until the dispute has been resolved. As a result, L should send C $70,000, which they have both agreed to, and can transfer $15,000 to her own account as part of her fees. The disputed $15,000 must remain in the client trust account until the dispute has been resolved.

As a side note, the ABA Rules encourage arbitration to resolve fee disputes, while the CA Rules mandate arbitration if the client demands it.

QUESTION 3: SELECTED ANSWER B

1.

Consensual Sexual Relationship

Under the ABA Model Rules (ABA), it is permissible for an attorney to represent a client with whom she has a pre-existing relationship, as long as the sexual relationship will not compromise the attorney's competence or duty of loyalty to the client. However, the ABA, lawyers may not enter into sexual relationships with clients that begin after they take on the clients. In California, attorneys may carry on sexual relationships that pre-existed the lawyer-client relationship, as well as being sexual relationships during the pendency of the representation, as long as competence and loyalty are not compromised. In addition, under CA rules, an attorney cannot condition acceptance of a client on agreement to have sex with the attorney. Here, the contractor and the lawyer had a preexisting sexual relationship, so their relationship did not automatically violate ABA or CA rules. However, the sexual relationship may have violated both ABA and CA rules because it conflicted with the duties of competence and loyalty (see below).

Duty of Competence

An attorney has a duty to competently represent her client which means using the knowledge, skill, thoroughness and preparation reasonably necessary for the representation. However, an attorney is permitted to take a case which she might not otherwise be competent to take if she can acquire through study the skills/knowledge necessary to represent the client and/or work with another attorney who specializes in that area.

Here, the attorney had never handled a complex construction defect case before. Thus, it appears she was not competent at the outset to do so. We have nothing in the facts to indicate that the attorney studied day and night to become reasonably competent to represent her client in this matter. And she did not partner with another attorney with expertise in construction defect cases.

Therefore, she violated her duty of competency when she agreed to represent contractor.

In addition, it appears that lawyer's pre-existing sexual relationship with client encouraged her to take a case for which she was not competent ("Lawyer felt pressured because of their relationship" may refer to taking the case as well as the fee she accepted.) Therefore, the lawyer also violated the duty not to let sexual relationships with clients interfere with your work, in violation of both ABA and CA rules.

Agreement not to sue for malpractice

Under ABA rules, a client can only contract away her right to sue an attorney for malpractice if the she is represented by outside counsel and agrees in writing. CA rules prohibit attorneys from contracting out of malpractice liability under any circumstances.

Here, Lawyer violated both ABA and CA rules. There is nothing on the facts to indicate that client was represented by outside counsel when he agreed not to sue for malpractice, or that the agreement was in writing. Thus, the ABA rules were violated. Because it is an agreement to limit malpractice liability the attorney violated CA law when she agreed to take on the case on this basis.

Duty of Loyalty

The duty of loyalty is always potentially implicated when a client and a lawyer have a sexual relationship. The duty of loyalty requires an attorney to avoid conflicts of interest. A conflict of interest exists when the interests of another client, a third party or the attorney herself are adverse to materially conflict with those of the client. Here, there is a potential conflict of interest between the lawyer's personal interest (her relationship with the client) and the representation. Under the ABA, when a conflict exists, an attorney can only represent a client if she reasonably believes she can do so competently, she discloses the conflict to the client, and gets the client's consent in writing. In CA, the belief need not be reasonable but only sincerely held, and personal conflicts only require written disclosure, not written, consent. Here, the attorney should have disclosed the nature of the potential conflict and gotten written consent at the outset (ABA). If she reasonably believed she could represent the client she could have done so with written consent, but here her belief would not be reasonable because she already felt pressured at the outset. Therefore, she violated ABA rules by taking on the case. Under CA rules, she would have had to provide only written disclosure (there is no indication of this on the facts) and the fact that her belief she could competently represent him would not matter. However, mere failure to provide written disclosure means that she already violated the CA duty of loyalty when she took the representation.

Fee agreement

Under the ABA, fee agreements must be reasonable. They don't have to be in writing, unless they are contingency agreements, in which case they must state the percentage of the attorney's fee, what expenses will be deducted, whether expenses will be deducted before the attorney's fee, and must be signed by the client. Under CA rules, all agreements over $1000, not with corporate clients, regular clients, or under exigent circumstances must be in writing. In addition to the ABA contingency fee requirements, CA contingency fees must include in writing that attorney fees are negotiable and state how non-covered services will be paid. In addition, the entire fee must not be unconscionable.

Here, attorney agreed to defend client at half her regular price, but his cross-complaint on a 30% contingency basis. Under ABA rules, the first part of the agreement did not need to be in writing but the second part did. There is no indication of a writing;

therefore the contingency agreement violated ABA rules. In addition, the agreement was probably per se unreasonable because it was the result of duress or undue influence exerted by the client.

Under CA rules, the whole agreement would have to be in writing unless they regularly worked together as lawyer-client or the first part was under $1000. Definitely the second contingency part had to be in writing, as it was not here, and lacked everything required in CA. In addition, despite the fact that 30% seems reasonable, it may be considered unconscionable because it was agreed to under duress and undue influence.

2. <u>Failure to make court appearance</u>

When the attorney failed to make the court appearance, she violated her duty of loyalty and competence to the client, and duty to pursue the case diligently. She didn't come to court due to what appears to be the deterioration of the sexual relationship. This means that she violated the duty not to let sexual relationships interfere with the representation, as well as the duty not to let her personal interests conflict with those of her client. In addition, she failed to pursue her case diligently in violation of her duty to her client and to the judicial system.

3. When there is a dispute over fees, the lawyer must retain the disputed portion in the client trust account pending resolution of the dispute. Here, the lawyer can send the 70k to the client, but must retain the additional 15k in the client trust account until the dispute is resolved.

QUESTION 4

Pop obtained a liability insurance policy from Insurco, covering his daughter Sally and any other driver of either of his cars, a Turbo and a Voka. The policy limit was $100,000.

On the application for the policy, Pop stated that his cars were driven in Hometown, a rural community, which resulted in a lower rate than if they were driven in a city. However, Sally kept and also drove the Voka in Industry City while attending college there.

Subsequently, Pop asked Insurco to increase his coverage to $500,000; Insurco agreed if he paid a premium increase of $150; and he did so. Days later, as he was leaving for Sally's graduation, Pop received an amended policy. He failed to notice that the coverage had been increased to $250,000, not $500,000.

Unfortunately, while driving the Turbo in Industry City, Pop caused a multi-vehicle collision. At first, Insurco stated it would pay claims, but only up to $250,000. Six months later, Insurco informed Pop that it would not pay any claim at all, because of his statement on the application for the policy that both the Turbo and the Voka were located in Hometown.

Insurco filed a complaint against Pop for rescission of the policy. Pop filed a cross-complaint to reform the policy to increase coverage to $500,000.

1. What is the likelihood of success of Insurco's complaint, and what defenses can Pop reasonably raise? Discuss.

2. What is the likelihood of success of Pop's cross-complaint, and what defenses can Insurco reasonably raise? Discuss.

QUESTION 4: SELECTED ANSWER A

(1) Likelihood of Success of Insurco's Complaint for Rescission

Rescission Generally

Rescission is an equitable remedy, under which a court will invalidate a contract in its entirety, such that the parties to the contract are completely excused from continued performance under the contract. Generally, rescission is available when one party has a valid defense to the formation of the contract. Moreover, typically only the wronged party can seek rescission.

Because rescission is an equitable remedy, a court has broad discretion in deciding whether it should be awarded. The court will consider the equities of the situation, taking into account the fairness of rescission to both parties. In addition, as an equitable remedy, rescission is subject to equitable defenses, such as acquiescence, estoppel, laches, and unclean hands.

Here, Insurco seeks rescission of the insurance policy so that it will not be required to reimburse Pop for his liability.

Insurco's Likely Grounds for Rescission

Fraud/Misrepresentation

Insurco's primary grounds for rescission will likely be on the basis of fraud. A contract may be invalid on the basis of fraud where: (1) a party made a false statement of past or present fact; (2) the statement was either fraudulent or was material to the contract; and (3) the other party relied on that statement of fact in entering into the contract.

Insurco can likely make out a claim of fraud under the facts of this case. Here, in applying for the liability insurance, Pop made a misstatement of fact--i.e., that his cars were driven solely in Hometown, a rural community. This was a false statement because one of his cars was driven by his daughter, Sally, in Industry City. Moreover, Pop was driving the other car in Industry City when he was involved in the collision.

Second, this statement may be deemed fraudulent, as it can probably be shown that Pop was aware of the falsity of the statement. It is very likely that Pop knew that the car was not being used solely in Hometown, as his daughter, Sally, used the car while she was attending college in Industry. Moreover, pop certainly knew that he was driving the Turbo in Industry City when he was involved in the accident.

Even if Insurco cannot establish that the statement was fraudulent, the elements of fraud are still likely established because it is clear that this statement was material to the contract. The location of the use of the cars appears to be a key factor in determining the insurance rates, and indeed, the facts make clear that Pop received a lower rate given this false statement of fact.

For this same reason, Insurco can establish that it relied on Pop's false statement in entering into the contract. As made clear in the facts, Insurco would not have entered into the contract at that lower rate, had it been aware that the car was used in Industry City.

Notably, this original contract is not the one Pop is intending to enforce. Rather, he is attempting to enforce the amended contract, in which Pop sought to increase his coverage. Because Pop paid consideration for this increase in coverage ($150), this modification of the contract is valid under the common law. In any event, this amended contract is subject to the same claim of rescission as the original contract, as there is no indication that Pop corrected his false statement when requesting the amended contract. Thus, Insurco's same arguments for establishing fraud discussed above apply equally with respect to the amended contract.

Accordingly, Insurco has a strong case for seeking rescission on the basis of fraud or misrepresentation.

Mistake

Insurco also may seek to rescind the contract on the basis of mistake. Under the doctrine of mutual mistake, a contract may be invalidated where both parties are mistaken about a material fact, that is, a fact that was a basic assumption of the contract. Under the doctrine of unilateral mistake, a contract may be invalidated where one party is mistaken about a material fact underlying the contract, and the other party knows or has reason to know about that mistake.

Here, to the extent Pop was unaware that Sally was using the car in Industry City, and somehow unaware that he was driving the car in Industry City when he entered into the accident, both he and Insurco were mistaken about this fact. Thus, the doctrine of mutual mistake of fact may be found to apply.

Moreover, to the extent Pop was aware of Sally's use of the car, or his use of the car in Industry City, he clearly also knew that Insurco would be mistaken as to this fact, given his false statement in applying for the insurance. Accordingly, under that scenario, the doctrine of unilateral mistake may apply. Note that unilateral mistake can serve as grounds for rescission of the contract only where the unmistaken party had actual knowledge of the other party's mistake.

However, because this situation involves a false statement of fact, this issue is more properly analyzed under the doctrine of fraud, for the reasons discussed above.

Pop's Likely Defenses

As noted above, a court will consider any equitable defenses before choosing to order rescission of a contract.

Laches

Pop will first rely on the equitable doctrine of laches. That defense applies where a claimant unreasonably delays in bringing suit, and where that suit prejudices the plaintiff.

Here, Pop will argue that Insurco's delay in bringing suit for rescission of the contract--six months after the accident, and even longer after Pop entered into the contract with Insurco--was unreasonable. The facts here are unclear as to the reasonableness of this delay, as it is not clear when Insurco became aware of Pop's misstatement. Given the fact that Pop's accident occurred in Industry City, however, there is a strong argument to be made that Insurco should have been aware of the use of Pop's cars in Industry City at the time Pop made his claim for reimbursement. Thus, Pop may be able to show the delay was unreasonable.

That said, there is no evidence that the Pop was prejudiced by the delay. Pop clearly will be prejudiced by not receiving payment for his liability, but there is no indication that the delay itself in seeking rescission caused Pop any harm. Thus, the defense of laches is likely unavailable.

Acquiescence

Pop may also rely on the equitable doctrine of acquiescence, which serves as a defense where the plaintiff has previously acquiesced to similar conduct on the part of the defendant for which the plaintiff is now seeking relief.

Here, Pop will argue that this defense is appropriate because Insurco has not previously objected to coverage on the basis of Pop's misstatement in applying for coverage, and that Insurco stated that it would pay his claims. However, Insurco will respond that it had no reason to be aware of Pop's misstatement until Pop sought reimbursement under the policy, and that this is the first time Pop has sought such reimbursement.

Insurco likely has the better argument here, given that it has never previously paid Pop under the policy in spite of the misrepresentation.

Unclean Hands

Unclean hands is an equitable defense available where the plaintiff has engaged in some wrongful or inequitable conduct with respect to the same underlying transaction for which the plaintiff is seeking relief.

Here, Pop may attempt to point to Insurco's previous statement that it would pay out on Pop's claim, and then its reversal of course. However, a court is unlikely to deem this inequitable or wrongful conduct, especially if Insurco was not aware of Pop's initial misstatement when it first agreed to pay Pop's claims.

Estoppel

Estoppel is an equitable defense available where a defendant reasonably, foreseeably, and detrimentally relied on a plaintiff's statement that the plaintiff's conduct is permissible, and where it is equitable to enforce that promise.

Pop will attempt to argue that Insurco is estopped from refusing to pay out on the claim, given its previous statement to Pop that it would reimburse him for his claim. However, there are no facts indicating that Pop relied on this promise to his detriment. Rather, the only harm Pop appears to have suffered is the fact that Insurco refuses to pay out on his claim. The facts do not indicate that Pop changed his position in any way in reasonable reliance on Insurco's promise itself.

Thus, this defense is unlikely to succeed.

(2) Likelihood of Success of Pop's Cross-Complaint for Reformation

Reformation Generally

Like rescission, reformation is also an equitable remedy. However, under the doctrine of reformation, a court will not invalidate the contract in its entirety, but rather will rewrite the contract to conform it to the parties' original intent. Moreover, like rescission, reformation is typically only available to the wronged party.

Again, because reformation is an equitable remedy, a court has broad discretion in deciding whether it should be awarded, taking account all of the equities. Reformation too is subject to equitable defenses, such as acquiescence, estoppel, laches, and unclean hands.

Pop's Likely Grounds for Reformation

Mistake

Pop will likely seek rescission on the doctrine of mutual mistake. As discussed above, that doctrine applies where both parties are mistaken about a material fact--i.e., a fact that was a basic assumption of the contract.

Here, the elements of that doctrine appear to apply. It seems that both parties intended that the amended contract increase the coverage limit to $500,000, as opposed to $250,000. In reducing the contract to writing, it appears that a clerical error was made, and that the contract was mistakenly written to state that the limit is $250,000. This appears to have been a mutual mistake, as the facts indicate that both parties initially intended that the limit be $500,000. Moreover, the mistake clearly regards a basic assumption of the contract, as a liability limit is one of the key elements of an insurance contract.

The doctrine does not apply where the party seeking to reform the contract assumed the risk of the mistake. That exception does not apply here, however, as it was Insurco, not Pop, who drafted the contract.

Accordingly, Pop has likely made out a prima facie case for mistake, and a court will likely reform the contract to make it consistent with the parties' intent that the liability limit be $500,000.

Insurco's Likely Defenses

Parol Evidence

Insurco may first rely on the parol evidence rule, which generally holds that where a contract is integrated (intended by the parties to be a final agreement), a party may not admit evidence of a prior agreement that is inconsistent with the contract's terms.

However, there is an exception to the parol evidence rule where a party seeks to provide evidence of mistake or clerical errors in reducing the contract to writing. This exception will apply here.

Unclean Hands

As noted above, the equitable defense of unclean hands applies where the plaintiff has engaged in some wrongful or inequitable conduct with respect to the same underlying transaction for which the plaintiff is seeking relief.

Here, Insurco has strong arguments for application of this defense, given that it can likely show that Pop fraudulently induced the contract. For the reasons discussed above, this claim will likely succeed. Accordingly, Pop's wrongful conduct in inducing the contract will likely serve as a defense to any claim for reformation.

Acquiescence and Laches

Insurco may also assert the defense of acquiescence and laches, the elements of which are discussed above.

With respect to both of these defenses, Insurco will argue Pop did not seek to reform the contract until many months after the amended policy went into effect, thus prejudicing Insurco. Insurco will focus on the fact that Pop had the policy in his possession at this time, and easily could have become aware of the mistake and sought reformation at an earlier time.

However, this argument is unlikely to be successful. A court will likely note that Insurco had a greater ability to have found the mistake, given that it was the party that reduced the contract to writing. Moreover, there do not appear to be facts indicating that Insurco was prejudiced by Pop's delay in seeking rescission.

QUESTION 4: SELECTED ANSWER B

1. INSURCO'S COMPLAINT

APPLICABLE LAW

The contract at issue is an insurance contract. UCC Article 2 governs sale of goods. All other contracts are governed by the common law. Accordingly, the common law would control.

RESCISSION

The issue in Insurco's complaint is whether it is entitled to rescission of the contract. The remedy of rescission allows the party asserting rescission to avoid its obligations under the contract. Rescission is allowed if there is a valid basis for rescission and there are no valid defenses. The remedy of rescission is meant to cure a problem that occurred during contract formation. Typical bases for rescission include: mutual mistake; unilateral mistake; fraudulent misrepresentation; misrepresentation of a material fact (even if not fraudulent); and ambiguous terms in the contract that neither party understood. The applicable bases for rescission in this case will be discussed in turn below.

A. Misrepresentation

Misrepresentation occurs when one party: (i) states a fact to the other party; (ii) the fact turns out to be false; (iii) the other party relied on the false statement when agreeing to enter the contract; and (iv) the party making the false statement either did so fraudulently, or the statement involved a material part of the contract (i.e., even if the statement was not made fraudulently, if it involved a material fact, that is still enough to make out a claim of misrepresentation).

Here, Insurco will argue that Pop made either a fraudulent or material misrepresentation in his application for insurance. In the application, Pop stated that his cars were driven in Hometown, which is a rural community that presumably has less traffic and less risk of accident than an urban center. In reality, however, one of the cars to be insured, the Voka, was also driven in Industry City by daughter while attending college. This made a difference to Insurco, as evidenced by its later refusal to pay once it realized that the application had only listed Hometown as the location of the cars, when in actuality the Voka was located much of the time in Industry City. The issue, however, is whether that discrepancy in the application was either fraudulently represented or material to the contract.

Fraud

There is no indication in the facts regarding whether Pop acted in good faith when he listed Hometown as the location of both cars. It is possible that Pop thought because the Turbo was always located in Hometown, and the Voka was only located in Industry City when college was in session, that he only needed to list Hometown. Pop would argue that Hometown was really the Voka's homebase, and that the car was only temporarily in Industry City for periods of time when college was in session.

Insurco would argue that Pop fraudulently listed only Hometown. Insurco would argue that anyone who drives a car knows that insurance rates go up in urban centers and will be lower in rural areas.

Based on the limited facts, Pop will likely prevail on the issue of fraud. Pop may still be on the hook for misrepresentation, however, if the fact at issue was material.

Materiality

A material fact is one that both parties needed to agree on for the contract to be valid--it is a term that cuts to the heart of what the contract is about. Here, the fact of where both cars were located most likely would be considered a material term. It would be considered a material term because the price of car insurance is affected greatly by where a car is driven. In urban centers the rates may be considerably higher than in rural areas. Accordingly, the fact of where the cars were located likely would be considered material.

Pop may argue it was an innocent mistake that he did not include Industry City in his application. Nonetheless, this is not a defense to mutual misrepresentation of a material fact. It does not matter whether the person who made the statement intended to defraud, it only matters whether they made an untrue statement of material fact.

Pop would further argue that he did not make an untrue statement. His statement that the cars were driven in Hometown was true, although incomplete. Although a party to a contract does not have a duty to disclose facts he is not asked about, he is not allowed to conceal facts or fail to disclose facts he is asked about. Here, Pop was asked in the application where the cars were located. By failing to answer the question completely, it is more likely a court would consider this a misrepresentation or concealment as opposed to a mere failure to disclose. Accordingly, Insurco can likely establish that the location of the cars was material.

Other Elements

In addition, Insurco can likely establish that Pop made a statement that turned out to be false regarding the location of the cars and that Insurco relied on that information when entering into the contract. As discussed above, Pop's intent is not what is at issue, it is only whether his answer turned out to be false. Here, the answer did turn out to be false because the Voka was also driven in Industry City.

Finally, Insurco also relied on the fact when it entered the contract. Insurco's rates were tied to the location of the cars. The fact that Insurco later refused to pay out the claim based on the location of the cars is evidence that it relied on the fact when entering into the contract.

Based on the above, Insurco can likely make out a claim of misrepresentation of a material fact. Thus, Insurco would be entitled to rescission unless Pop raises a valid defense.

B. Mutual Mistake

Mutual mistake occurs when both parties to a contract made a mistake regarding a material term of the contract on which the contract was based. For a party to successfully assert mutual mistake, that party must not have assumed the risk of the mistake occurring. A classic example of mutual mistake was the case involving the sale of a cow that both parties believed was barren, but that later turned out to be able to have children. In that case the two parties made a contract for the sale of a barren cow. The fact that the cow was barren was a mistake that involved a material issue that the contract was based on. In that case, if the seller could have easily had the cow examined to find out whether it was actually barren, then the seller assumed the risk and would not be able to assert mutual mistake.

Here, Insurco would argue that even if it cannot establish the misrepresentation discussed above, it can establish mutual mistake. The mutual mistake would be the fact of where the cars were driven. It was a mistake from Pop's end because he mistakenly forgot to include the fact that the Voka was driven in Industry City. It was a mistake from Insurco's end because it mistakenly thought the cars were driven only in Hometown even though the Voka was also driven in Industry City.

This argument is weaker than the misrepresentation argument. Here, Insurco's mistake was not really based on the terms in the offer or acceptance, but instead was based on Pop failing to disclose information. Mutual mistake usually applies in situations where a fact in the offer or acceptance turns out to be different than both parties thought. Here,

Pop knew the Voka was driven in Industry City, and Insurco did not know because Pop failed to disclose that information. Accordingly, mutual mistake is not as strong an argument for Insurco as misrepresentation.

C. Unilateral Mistake

Unilateral mistake can serve as a basis for rescission when one party made a mistake in the contract formation that the other party knew or should have known about. The typical example arises when many subcontractors are bidding for a construction contract and one subcontractor's bid is so low that the general contractor should know that the subcontractor made an error in its bid. In such a situation, the subcontractor who made the error can rescind the contract based on unilateral mistake because the general contractor knew or should have known of the mistake. In unilateral mistake, the negligence of the party that made the mistake is not a defense to rescission of the contract.

Here, Insurco would argue that it made a unilateral mistake in issuing the insurance policy under rates applicable only to Hometown. Further, Pop knew or should have known of the error. It appears Pop reviewed the initial policy because he requested an increase in coverage. Accordingly, Pop should have known that there was a mistake in the initial policy based on Insurco's misunderstanding of where the cars were located.

Unilateral mistake is a difficult claim to make out, and Insurco would likely not succeed in this argument. The doctrine would be more applicable if Insurco made a mistake in information it provided to Pop. Here, the real issue is information Pop provided to Insurco. Accordingly, misrepresentation is a stronger basis for Insurco's argument.

D. Ambiguity

If a term in contract formation is ambiguous, such that it is open to multiple interpretations, then one of the parties to the contract can later avoid the contract based on that ambiguity. The classic example of ambiguity is the case of the Peerless, where one party thought the shipment referred to the November Peerless, and the other party thought the shipment referred to the December Peerless. In that case, because the term Peerless was open to multiple meanings, it was considered ambiguous, and the party was able to avoid the contract as a result. However, if one party knows that the ambiguous term could refer to multiple interpretations, then that party is charged with knowledge and the unknowing party can enforce the contract based on what it believed the ambiguous term to mean.

Here, Insurco would argue that the term regarding where the cars were driven was ambiguous. The term was ambiguous because Pop understood the term to refer only to where the cars were located much of the time, whereas Insurco believed the term to refer to where the cars were located all of the time. Under such an argument, Insurco would claim that because Pop had reason to know that the Voka was driven in Industry City as well, Pop was the party with knowledge, and the contract should be construed against Pop to Insurco's benefit.

This argument is also a difficult one. Usually ambiguous terms refer to the word itself. Here, the word "Hometown" was not ambiguous. What was ambiguous was the question on the application of where the cars were located. If Insurco can establish that the question was ambiguous to the point it led to miscommunication, then it may be able to succeed in its argument. Still, the stronger claim for Insurco is misrepresentation.

E. Defenses

Rescission is an equitable remedy, so equitable defenses apply. The defenses of unclean hands and laches are the most common. Unclean hands refers to the plaintiff taking inequitable actions regarding the contract itself. Laches refers to an unreasonable delay in bringing a claim that prejudices the defendant.

Laches

Here, Pop would argue that the claim for rescission is barred by laches. After the accident, Insurco agreed to pay out the $250,000. Only six months later, did Insurco inform Pop it would not pay the claim at all. Pop would argue the six month delay was unreasonable. After the accident occurred, Insurco had all the information it needed to make its decision about paying the claim. If Insurco intended not to pay out the claim, it should have made that clear right away after the accident. By waiting six months, Pop and Sally were prejudiced by the delay. They likely incurred many costs associated with the accident, and were depending on the insurance payout to be able to cover those costs.

Insurco would counter that it was unable to ascertain the fact that the Voka was located in Industry City until doing in-depth investigation. The facts do not state how Insurco ultimately learned the Voka had been located in Industry City. If it is true that that information was difficult to find out, then Insurco has a good argument for the delay. If, however, it was easily ascertainable that the car was located in Industry City, Insurco's argument is weaker.

Because rescission is an extreme remedy here given the damage in the accident and also given that the most Insurco is willing to pay out is only $250,000 and not $500,000, the court would likely not find rescission to be the appropriate remedy.

2. POP'S CROSS-COMPLAINT

Pop's cross-complaint asserts a claim to reform the contract to allow for the full $500,000 in coverage. For reformation to be available, there must be a valid contract, grounds for reformation, and no valid defense. Reformation is typically ordered in situations where both parties agreed to certain terms of the contract, and those terms did not end up in the finalized contract due to an error such as a scrivener's error.

Here, Pop will argue that he and Insurco made a valid contract modification to increase the coverage of the insurance policy from $100,000 to $500,000. For a contract modification to be valid, there must be consideration for the modification. Here, there was $150 in consideration paid, and as a result, both Pop and Insurco agreed that the coverage would be increased to $500,000. Here, Pop paid the additional $150, and at that point the agreement was complete and the modification should have been for coverage of $500,000.

Pop will further argue that even though there was a valid modification, the increase was only to $250,000. Pop will claim this must have been due to a scrivener's error or some other error, because the agreement he had made with Insurco before receiving the amended policy was clear.

Based on the facts, Pop has a strong argument for reformation of the contract because it appears that the clear intent of the parties was to modify the contract for $500,000 coverage, and Pop complied with his end of the bargain by paying the $150.

Defenses

Lack of Initial Contract

Insurco can argue that reformation is not permitted because there was never a valid contract in the first place. For reformation to be a possible remedy, there first must have been a valid contract. Insurco would assert the same arguments discussed above regarding contract formation (i.e., mistake, misrepresentation, ambiguity) to argue there never was a valid contract in the first place, and therefore reformation is not allowed.

Parol Evidence

Insurco would also argue that the oral agreement between Pop and Insurco regarding the increase in coverage is inadmissible under the parol evidence rule. Under the parol evidence rule, if there is a final, fully integrated contract, then any communications regarding the contract terms that contradict or supplement the contract either before or contemporaneous with the contract being finalized are inadmissible.

Here, Insurco would argue that the amended policy was a final integration of the contract, and that any evidence of what happened leading up to the amendment is inadmissible parol evidence.

Pop would counter that because the agreement served as the basis for the contract itself, it would not be considered parol evidence, but rather was the basis for the entire modification. Based on the facts, however, it appears the amended policy was a final integrated contract. Accordingly, Pop's arguments would likely fail.

Unclean Hands

Finally, Insurco could assert a defense of unclean hands. Insurco would argue that Pop intentionally misled Insurco into believing the two cars were located solely in Hometown, when in reality the Voka was located in Industry City. Insurco would make similar arguments as discussed above in its claim for rescission. Ultimately Pop would probably prevail on this argument, because there is no evidence he acted in bad faith.

Conclusion

The court would probably not grant Pop's claim for reformation of the contract because of the parol evidence rule. However, they could probably also not grant Insurco's claim for rescission. Acting in equity, the court would most likely find that the contract for $250,000 of coverage controlled.

QUESTION 5

Mike, Sue, Pam, David, and Ed worked at Ace Manufacturing Company. Mike had been the president and Sue supervised Pam, David, and Ed.

Pam was fired. A week later, David circulated the following email to all the other employees:

> I just thought you should know that Pam was fired because she is a thief. Sue caught her stealing money from the petty cash drawer after Pam's affair with Mike ended.

A month later, Mike died.

Pam sued David for defamation.

At trial, Pam testified that, although it is true she was fired, the remaining contents of the email were false. Pam called Ed, who testified that he had received the email at work, that he had printed it, and that he had received hundreds of other unrelated emails from David. Pam introduced a copy of the email through Ed.

In defense, David called Sue, who testified that she had caught Pam stealing $300 from the petty cash drawer, and that, when Sue confronted Pam and accused her of taking the money, Pam simply walked away. David himself testified that the contents of the email were true. He also testified that he had overheard Pam and Mike yelling at each other in Mike's office a few weeks before Pam left; that he recognized both of their voices; and that he heard Pam cry, "Please don't leave me!," and Mike, in a measured tone, reply, "Our affair is over — you need to get on with your life."

Assume all appropriate objections were timely made.

Should the court have admitted:

1. The email? Discuss.

2. Sue's testimony? Discuss.

3. David's testimony about

   a. what Pam said to Mike? Discuss.

   b. what Mike said to Pam? Discuss.

Answer according to the California Evidence Code.

QUESTION 5: SELECTED ANSWER A

Because this is a civil case, Proposition 8 does not apply.

1. The email

The issue is whether the court properly admitted the email.

Relevance

The first question is whether the email was relevant. Under the California Evidence Code (CEC), evidence is relevant if it tends to make an issue of consequence (a material fact) more or less probable. In other words, evidence must be material and probative (although the level of probativity is very low--it must only affect probability to a slight degree). Under the California rule, the issue must be actually disputed (this is different than the Federal Rules). Relevance is in general a low bar.

Here, the email is relevant. First, it is relevant to the issue of whether the allegedly defamatory statements were made at all. It is also relevant to the question of publication. Defamation requires publication (dissemination) of a statement to a third party. Here, the existence of the email is relevant (although the printing of the email was not necessary for publication). There may be some argument that the issue of the statement and the publication are not disputed, but this would probably not succeed, especially given that under the secondary evidence rule, the email itself should be admitted rather than mere testimony as to its contents.

The next issue is whether the relevance is substantially outweighed by the likelihood of unfair prejudice. It is important to note that any prejudice must be unfair--any evidence counter to a party's case will be prejudicial. The prejudice must actually be unfair--the type that would unduly influence a finder of fact. Here, it is highly unlikely that the email would be found to be unfairly prejudicial.

Authentication/Foundation

The next question is whether the email was properly authenticated/whether a proper foundation for introduction of the email was made. Here, the email has likely been properly authenticated. Ed testified that he has personal knowledge of the email--he received it. Moreover, his testimony that he had received hundreds of other emails from David supports a finding that the email did in fact come from David. It should be noted that the evidence need not be proven to be conclusively authentic. Rather, a jury must be able to conclude that the email is authentic.

Hearsay

Next, there could be an argument from David that the email is inadmissible hearsay. Hearsay is an out-of-court statement offered to prove the truth of the matter asserted. Here, the email is an out-of-court statement made by David. However, it is not being offered for the truth of the matter asserted. The email is not being introduced to prove its contents (Pam is in fact arguing the email was false). The email is of independent legal significance--the fact that the statement was made is relevant to the cause of action. Moreover, even if the email were hearsay, it would be admissible under the exception for statements of a party-opponent (California does not make party-opponent statements exempted from hearsay; they merely fall under an exception).

Therefore, the email was properly admitted.

2. Sue's testimony

Relevance

The first issue is whether the testimony is relevant, under the standard recited above. Here, Sue's testimony is relevant to the issue of whether the contents of the email were truthful, which is an issue disputed in the case. Her testimony makes it more probable that the email is true (as compared to the likelihood without her testimony). And there does not appear to be any unfair prejudice that would substantially outweigh the relevance.

Foundation

The next issue is whether Sue has personal knowledge and the proper foundation has been laid. Here, Sue is testifying based on her own personal knowledge that she saw Pam stealing. Therefore, the proper foundation exists.

Character Evidence

Pam may object to the evidence being introduced as character evidence. Normally, character evidence is not admissible in civil cases. An exception applies when character is at issue. Here, Pam's character is at issue. Her argument is that the email was false. Therefore, whether Pam embezzled or not is directly at issue, and evidence on embezzlement is relevant and admissible. Therefore, Sue's testimony that she had seen Pam stealing money from the cash drawer is not inadmissible as character evidence.

Hearsay

Pam may also argue that the testimony about her walking away is inadmissible hearsay. As discussed above, hearsay is an out-of-court statement offered to prove the truth of the matter above. "Statements" can include assertive conduct, such as nodding or hand gestures. Here, Pam would argue that her walking away was an assertive act and therefore a statement. It is questionable as to whether her act in walking away is a statement. But even if it is, here the statement is admissible under the hearsay exception for party-opponent statements. Pam is a party to the lawsuit and she is David's opponent (David is offering the testimony).

Pam could further try to attack Sue's testimony that she "accused [Pam] of taking the money" as inadmissible hearsay. It is unclear exactly how Sue's testimony was phrased. However, even if the testimony did constitute an out-of-court statement, David has several arguments for admitting the testimony. First, he could argue that Pam adopted the statement and that therefore it falls under the party-opponent statement. A statement is adopted where a person could reasonably be expected to respond to a statement but does not. Here, David would argue that Pam could reasonably be expected to deny the accusation and that her silence and walking away adopts Sue's statement. However, this is not a typical situation where the adopted statement theory would apply, since it is unlikely that Pam would adopt a statement that she had stolen the money. There could also be an argument that the statement is not hearsay at all because it is not being offered to prove the content of Sue's statement. For example, it could be argued that the statement is being offered to show its effect on Pam (although this argument does not seem particularly strong). It could also be argued that the statement goes to a fact of independent significance, since it shows the fact that Sue caught Pam stealing money (as asserted in the email).

It seems most likely that this testimony was not recounting an out-of-court statement at all, and was merely discussing Sue's action. But the other arguments above may also allow admission, even if it is testimony of an out-of-court statement.

David could also argue that, if it were determined that Pam had adopted Sue's statement, it was a prior inconsistent statement (Pam testified that the email was false), and that therefore the statement was admissible under the CEC for both impeachment and to show the truth of the matter asserted. However, as discussed above, the argument that Pam adopted the statements seems likely to succeed.

Overall, the court was likely correct in admitting the testimony.

3. David's testimony

The next issue relates to David's testimony.

a. Pam's statements to Mike

Relevance

As to Pam's statements to Mike, the first issue is relevance. This testimony is relevant because it again goes to whether the contents of the email were true. With the testimony, it is more likely than without the testimony that the email's contents about David's and Pam's relationship is true. Pam could argue that her statement by itself does not establish that there was any relationship--it was ambiguous. But, the evidence need not be sufficient to establish the ultimate fact at issue. Instead, it merely needs to make the likelihood that there was an affair (a disputed issue) more probable than it would be without the evidence. The testimony here clears that low bar. And again, there does not seem to be any unfair prejudice that would substantially outweigh the relevance.

Foundation

The second question is foundation. David testified that he recognized Pam's voice. Without more, that assertion may not be enough to show foundation and personal knowledge. But if David were to testify, for example, that he had long worked with Pam and had previously heard her voice, the foundation would likely be sufficient.

Hearsay

Pam may attempt to argue that this testimony is inadmissible hearsay. The statement is likely hearsay--it was an out-of-court statement. And it is being offered to show that Pam made that statement to Mike (because they were having an affair). But this statement falls into the party-opponent exception for hearsay. Even if it did not, it may also fall under the excited utterance exception since Pam's emotions seem to have been aroused the time of her statement. A witness need not be unavailable for that exception to apply.

Moreover, David could argue that this statement is admissible as a prior inconsistent statement. Pam testified that the email was false. David could argue that this statement was a previous inconsistent statement, which under the California Evidence Code would be admissible for both impeachment purposes and to show the truth of the matter asserted.

b. Mike's statements to Pam

The next issue is whether the court previously admitted David's testimony about what Mike said to Pam.

Relevance

The first question is relevance. As discussed above, the question of whether there was an affair is at issue in the case because Pam is arguing falsity of the email. David's testimony about Mike's statements makes it more likely that the email was true than without his testimony. Again, the testimony need not conclusively establish truth. Rather, it must only make it more likely than it would be without the evidence. Mike's statement is even more clearly relevant than Pam's statement, since it explicitly references an affair.

Foundation

The next issue is whether David testified with the appropriate foundation and personal knowledge. As mentioned above, Pam may argue that David lacked the foundation to testify based on only hearing the voices rather than actually seeing the argument.

Without any testimony as to how David knew that Mike was speaking, the proper foundation is probably lacking. But if David were able to testify that he had previously heard Mike's voice, there would be a proper foundation. Moreover, the fact that the conversation was overheard from Mike's office would support the identification of Mike. Again, it need not be conclusively proven that it was Mike's voice. It just needs to be enough to support a verdict.

Opinion Evidence

Pam could potentially argue that David offered improper opinion evidence when he said that Mike replied in "a measured tone." Lay opinion testimony is admissible if it is 1) based on the witness's perception, 2) helpful, and 3) did not require any specialized knowledge. Here, David has a strong argument that his statement that Mike responded in a measured tone is helpful to provide context to the jury and to show the affair (if David were mad, for example, it could be argued that his statements were false or made in the heat of passion). This testimony as to the tone of voice is probably admissible.

Hearsay

The crux of whether the statement is admitted is likely whether it is inadmissible hearsay. Here, there was an out-of-court statement made by Mike. And it is likely being offered for the truth of the matter asserted--that there was an affair (see below for an argument that it is not hearsay). Therefore, the question is whether it falls under the California exceptions.

California has a hearsay exception for dying declarations in all civil and criminal cases. But Mike's statement does not satisfy that exception. True, Mike is dead, as is required by the California exception. But Mike did not make the statement as his death was impending and it does not relate to the cause of his death.

This also is not an excited utterance--Mike replied in a measured tone. This is not a statement of past or present physical or mental condition (although Mike would satisfy the unavailability requirement). And this is not a statement where Mike is describing his current actions.

David may have a good argument that this is a statement against interest. Under the federal rules, a statement is against interest if it is against penal or pecuniary interest. California also applies the exception where the statement is against social interest. The witness must be unavailable. Here, Mike satisfies the unavailability requirement (he is dead). And this statement could be found to be against social interest. Mike's statement that he was having an affair could be seen as exposing him to adverse social judgments. This would be David's best exception for a hearsay exception to apply.

David could also attempt to argue that this was not hearsay at all because, while it is an out-of-court statement, it is not being offered to prove the truth of the matter asserted. Rather, David could attempt to show that it was being introduced to show its effect on him, the listener. This argument may not be successful because it would be questionable whether such evidence would be relevant. In a defamation case, truth is a defense. But it is not clear that David's state of mind is relevant. If Sue and/or Mike were public figures or if the matter were one of public interest, then David's state of mind would be relevant, since fault would need to be shown. But if fault need not be shown, then the statement may not be admissible for its effect on him. If the statement were admitted for such a purpose, a limiting instruction would likely be given.

David could also attempt to argue against inadmissibility by arguing that this statement is being used for impeachment purposes, since Pam testified. However, the out-of-court statement of another person is generally not admissible to impeach.

Overall, the best argument is that this was not hearsay or, even better, was a statement against interest. It seems that the testimony was very likely properly admitted.

QUESTION 5: SELECTED ANSWER B

California Evidence Code & Truth in Evidence (Prop 8)

The California Evidence Code (CEC) governs the admission of evidence in California state courts. A constitutional amendment called the Truth in Evidence Amendment (Prop 8) was passed in the 1980s. Prop 8 applies only in criminal cases. It provides that all relevant evidence in California is admissible notwithstanding CEC rules to the contrary. Prop 8 has a number of exclusions, however: (1) hearsay rules; (2) the confrontation clause; (3) CEC 352 (balancing test); (4) privileges; (5) character evidence; (6) the secondary evidence rule.

Because this is a civil lawsuit and not a criminal lawsuit, Prop 8 does not apply.

1. The Email

- *Logical relevance*

In order for evidence to be admissible, it must be logically relevant. That means that it must have the tendency to make any fact of consequence to the dispute more or less probable than without the evidence. Under the CEC, the fact must also be in dispute. Here, the email is logically relevant because it constitutes the basis of the lawsuit and is actually in dispute.

- *Legal relevance*

In order for evidence to be admissible, it must also be legally relevant, as tested under CEC 352. In order to be legally relevant, the probative value of the evidence must not be substantially outweighed by undue prejudice, waste of time, or confusion. In addition, there must not be any policy exclusions that might apply to prevent introduction of the evidence (such as prior offers to settle, etc.). Here, the email is legally relevant because its probative value--whether it supports a case for defamation--is not outweighed by undue prejudice, waste of time, or confusion.

- *Authentication*

In order for relevant tangible evidence to be admissible, it must also be authenticated. The standard for testing this is whether it is sufficient to sustain a finding of authenticity. A number of different kinds of authentication evidence are permissible: (1) personal knowledge; (2) circumstantial evidence; (3) expert testimony; (4) admission, etc. Here, Ed introduced the email. He testified that he had received the email at work and printed it, and that he had received hundreds of other unrelated emails from David. While it would be preferable to have David authenticate the mail he wrote, this authentication is likely sufficient to sustain a finding of authenticity.

- *Secondary Evidence Rule*

When the contents of a writing are at the heart of the matter, the secondary evidence rule requires that either an original or duplicate of the document be introduced into evidence (or testimony where the original is unavailable). In California, a duplicate can be: (1) photocopy; (2) carbon copy; or (3) handwritten copy (not true in FRE). Here, the contents of the email are relevant to defamation cause of action. This printing of the email is essentially a photocopy and would satisfy the secondary evidence rule.

- *Independent Legal Significance*

Pam might argue that the email is not hearsay because it has independent legal significance. Indeed, because this is a defamation action and the email is the defamatory statement, this is likely to be successful.

- *Layered Hearsay*

Hearsay is an out-of-court statement offered for the truth of the matter asserted. It is generally inadmissible unless it falls within an exception. (The FRE has both exemptions and exceptions, but the CEC only has exceptions.) Here, if the email were not admitted as having independent legal significance, the email is layered hearsay so both the email itself and the statement contained therein must fall admissible under an exception.

- *Email: Business Record*

A business record is: (1) a recording of an event or condition; (2) made by someone with personal knowledge; (3) made at or near the time the event; (4) kept in the ordinary course of business. Here, the email would not qualify as a business record because David was under no business duty to send this email.

- *Statements in Email: Admission by Party Opponent*

A statement being offered against a party is an admission by a party opponent. The statement need not have been against the party's interest at the time it was made to qualify. Here, David's statement is being offered against him, and thus it would be admissible as an admission by a party opponent.

- *Conclusion*

The email will be admissible because it has independent legal significance and is thus not hearsay.

2. Sue's Testimony

• *Logical Relevance*

See rule above. This evidence is logically relevant because it has the tendency to make a fact of consequence that is in dispute (whether Pam is a thief) more or less probable.

• *Legal Relevance*

See rule above. This evidence is legally relevant because its probative value--whether Pam is a thief--is not outweighed by undue prejudice, waste of time, or confusion. Pam may argue that this is unduly prejudicial because it paints her as a thief, but she has asserted that the statement in the email is false, and thus the court will allow it.

• *Competence*

For a witness to be competent to testify, she must have personal knowledge, present recollection, the ability to communicate, and understand that she is under a legal duty to tell the truth. These factors appear to be met -- Sue has personal knowledge of her interaction with Pam and appears to have a present recollection of the interaction. Furthermore, there is nothing to indicate that she lacks the ability to communicate or that she doesn't understand her legal duty to tell the truth. Sue is competent to testify.

• *Character Evidence: Pam Stealing $300 of Petty Cash*

Character evidence is evidence that tends to convey a moral judgment about someone. The testimony about Pam stealing $300 from the petty cash drawer is character evidence. In California, character evidence in civil cases is inadmissible to prove circumstantial evidence of guilt (there are no exceptions like under the FRE). However, character evidence is admissible if it is in issue, as is the case here. This is a defamation case where Pam has alleged that David's statement calling her a thief is false. Therefore, evidence of her being a thief is highly probative and directly in issue. Thus, the court will allow Sue's testimony that Pam stole $300 of petty cash.

[Note that this could also be considered impeachment evidence. Pam has testified that the contents of the email were false. Specific incidents can be used to impeach a witness, and this would also be appropriate impeachment evidence.]

- *Sue's statement accusing Pam of Taking the Money: Not Hearsay*

Sue's statement accusing Pam of taking the money is not hearsay because it is not being offered for the truth of the matter asserted. Instead, it is being offered to show its effect on the listener (Pam).

- *Sue's statement that Pam walked away: Hearsay*

Sue also seeks to testify about Pam walking away when accused of a crime. This statement is hearsay. Hearsay encompasses all assertive conduct, which is conduct that is intended to communicate something. Thus, unless it falls within a hearsay exception, this statement which is being offered for the truth of the matter asserted (that she would not have walked away if she weren't guilty) is hearsay.

- *Admission by Party Opponent: Adoptive Admission*

A statement being offered against a party is an admission by a party opponent. The statement need not have been against the party's interest at the time it was made to qualify. Adoptive admissions occur where a party is accused or confronted and we would expect them to deny a statement but instead they remain silent, implicitly adopting the statement. Here, we would expect an innocent party accused of stealing to defend herself if it were not true. By simply walking away, Pam has adopted the statement.

- *Conclusion*

Sue's testimony about Pam stealing $300 of petty cash is admissible because it is character evidence that is in issue in a defamation case; her statement to Pam accusing her of taking the money is not hearsay because it is offered to show its effect on the listener; her statement about Pam's reaction is admissible as an adoptive admission by a party opponent.

3a. David's Testimony About What Pam Said to Mike

- *Logical Relevance*

See rule above. This evidence is logically relevant because it relates to whether Pam was having an affair with Mike, a key subject of the defamation action and one that is hotly contested.

- *Legal Relevance*

See rule above. This evidence is legally relevant because its probative value--whether Pam was having an affair with Mike--is not outweighed by undue prejudice, waste of time, or confusion.

- *Authentication*

In order for this testimony to be admissible, David must be able to authenticate that it was, indeed, Pam speaking. The standard for testing this is whether it is sufficient to sustain a finding of authenticity. Here, David is presumably familiar with Pam's voice and has heard it many times before. This will be adequate to sustain a finding of authenticity.

- *Hearsay*

See rule above. This evidence is being offered to prove the truth of the matter asserted (i.e., that Pam was having an affair with Mike). Thus, unless an exception applies, it is inadmissible.

- *Hearsay Exception: Admission by Party Opponent*

A statement being offered against a party is an admission by a party opponent. This statement, made by Pam, is being offered against her. It is thus admissible as an admission by a party opponent.

- *Hearsay Exception: Excited Utterance*

An excited utterance is a statement made relating to a startling event or condition made while under the stress or excitement of that event or condition. A declarant's availability is irrelevant. Here, Pam cried in what appears to be an excited voice: "Please don't leave me!" This may qualify as an excited utterance, but the better fit is an admission by a party opponent.

- *No privileges*

Because Pam and David are not married, there are no privileges that might apply to this otherwise confidential communication.

- *Conclusion*

This testimony is admissible as an admission by a party opponent.

3b. David's Testimony About What Mike Said to Pam

- *Logical Relevance*

See rule above. This evidence is logically relevant because it relates to whether Pam was having an affair with Mike, a key subject of the defamation action and one that is hotly contested.

- *Legal Relevance*

See rule above. This evidence is logically relevant because it relates to whether Pam was having an affair with Mike, a key subject of the defamation action and one that is hotly contested.

- *Authentication*

See rule above. Here, David is presumably familiar with Mike's voice and has heard it many times before. This will be adequate to sustain a finding of authenticity.

- *Hearsay*

See rule above. This evidence is being offered to prove the truth of the matter asserted (i.e., that Pam was having an affair with Mike). Thus, unless an exception applies, it is inadmissible.

- *Declaration Against Interest*

A declaration against interest is a statement made by an unavailable declarant that was against his interest at the time it was made and that the declarant knew was against his interest at the time it was made. In California, it can be against a person's penal, financial, or social interest. A statement is against someone's social interest if it would subject them to hatred, ridicule, or disgust. Declarations against interest are only admissible where a declarant is unavailable. A declarant can be unavailable due to death, inability to secure their presence through reasonable process, total memory failure, privileges, or their refusal to testify out of fear and despite a court order.

Here, Mike died and is thus unavailable. The statement by Mike ("Our affair is over") is against his social interest. He was acknowledging that he was having an affair with Pam in the first place. Thus the first part of his statement "Our affair is over" is admissible as a declaration against interest.

- *Dying Declaration*

A dying declaration is a statement made by a declarant while he thought he was imminently dying and describing the conditions or circumstances of his death. The declarant must be unavailable, and in California the declarant must have actually died and it can be used in either civil or criminal cases. This statement does not appear to be while David thought he was dying or about the conditions and circumstances surrounding his death. It is thus inadmissible as a dying declaration.

- *Excited Utterance*

See rule above. This exception does not apply because the facts state that David responded "in a measured tone." Therefore, he was not under the stress or excitement of an event.

- *Present State of Mind*

A statement describing a person's present state of mind (usually statements like "I intend" or "I plan") are admissible as hearsay exceptions regardless of the declarant's availability. Here, the first part of the statement may also qualify under the present state of mind exception because it is demonstrating that David intends to end the affair. Nonetheless, the declaration against interest exception is the best fit for this statement.

- *No privileges*

Because Pam and David are not married, there are no privileges that might apply to this otherwise confidential communication.

- *Conclusion*

This testimony "Our affair is over" is admissible as a declaration against interest. The second half of the testimony "you need to get on with your life" may be admissible only if it is being offered to show the effect on the listener, Pam.

QUESTION 6

On February 1, Bing Surfboards ("Bing") ordered 400 gallons of epoxy from Super Chemicals ("Super") using its standard purchase order. Bing's purchase order provided that delivery would be no later than February 20, but stated nothing about warranties, disclaimers, or remedies. Super responded with its standard acknowledgment, which purported to accept the order and confirmed that delivery would be no later than February 20. It also provided: (1) "Seller disclaims all warranties of merchantability and fitness." (2) "In no event shall Seller be liable for consequential damages." (3) "This acceptance is expressly made conditional on your assent to the terms of this acceptance."

On February 15, Bing received the epoxy.

On February 20, Bing tested the epoxy by manufacturing 50 surfboards. The epoxy did not harden properly, leaving the surfboards useless.

On February 23, Bing emailed Super stating that the epoxy had failed to harden properly and that it was returning the remaining epoxy.

On February 25, not having heard from Super, Bing bought 400 gallons of epoxy from one of Super's competitors, paying a substantially higher price for quick delivery, which was necessary to avoid a shutdown of Bing's production line.

On February 26, Super informed Bing that it was shipping replacement epoxy to arrive the following day. The original epoxy had failed to harden because of manufacturing defects of which Super was unaware. Although the replacement epoxy was not defective, Bing rejected delivery and refused to pay.

Bing has sued Super for the increased price of epoxy it had to pay to Super's competitor, and for loss due to 50 defective surfboards.

Super has sued Bing for rejecting its replacement shipment and for not paying under the contract.

1. Is Bing likely to prevail in its suit? Discuss.

2. Is Super likely to prevail in its suit? Discuss.

QUESTION 6: SELECTED ANSWER A

Bing's suit against Super

Governing law

The contract in question concerns epoxy, a good. Thus, UCC Article 2 applies to the contract.

Both Bing and Super are merchants, since Bing deals usually in surfboards and Super deals usually in epoxy and other chemicals. Thus, the rules applicable are those where both parties to the contract are merchants.

Contract formation

An initial question is whether a contract was formed by Super's standard acknowledgment.

In order for a valid contract to be formed, there must be offer, acceptance and consideration. Under the UCC, conditional acceptance is not treated as an acceptance; rather it is treated as a rejection. Here, Super's response to Bing was clearly conditional. Thus, it functioned as a rejection of Bing's offer, and no contract was formed.

Although no contract was formed, a subsequent implied contract may nevertheless have been formed by the performance of the parties. Here, Super did indeed send epoxy to Bing, which accepted it and, at least initially, did not object. All of the subsequent conduct and communications of Bing and Super are also in line with the existence of a contract. Thus, it is possible that the court will find an implied contract between the parties. Such a contract, implied purely from conduct, would not contain any of the disclaimers in Super's acknowledgment form. Thus, default warranties and damages rules would apply.

Terms of the contract

Even if the court instead finds that a contract was formed by Super's acknowledgment, it is likely Bing can show that the terms regarding disclaimer of warranties and consequential damages have not been integrated into the contract.

Under UCC, for a contract between two merchants, offer does not have to mirror acceptance. However, any terms in the acceptance that vary the offer will not become a part of the contract unless (1) both parties are merchants, (2) the terms are not material, and (3) no objection is raised to them within a reasonable time.

Here, both the disclaimer or warranties and the limitation of damages are material terms, since the warranties go to the heart of the quality of goods being delivered and the limitation of damages speak directly to the economic interests of the parties. Since one of the elements is not met, these terms are not part of the contract, and the default warranties and damages rules apply.

Perfect Tender

Bing is likely able to demonstrate that a perfect tender was not made by Super, entitling it to reject the goods and cease performance (also relevant to Super's suit, later) and seek alternative goods.

Under the UCC, failure to make a perfect tender of goods ordered is a breach of the contract that allows the non-breaching party to reject goods and cease performance. Also, a warranty of merchantability is implied if the seller is a merchant, stating that the goods are fit for their ordinary purpose, and a warranty of fitness is implied if the seller knows the buyer is buying the goods for a particular purpose and relying on seller to provide conforming goods. (As noted above, these warranties have not been properly disclaimed.)

Here, it would appear likely that both warranties are breached. The warranty of merchantability is breached since the epoxy was defective due to a manufacturing problem - unless it can be shown that the defect affects surfboards but not the usual uses of epoxy, the warranty is breached. The warranty of fitness is breached since Super knew Bing needed the epoxy for surfboards (because Bing's name is Bing Surfboards) and was relying on Super to deliver the epoxy fit for the manufacturing of surfboards, and failed to deliver that kind of epoxy.

Since the epoxy delivered was nonconforming goods that did not satisfy the implied warranties, perfect tender was not made.

(Note: If the warranties were in fact properly disclaimed from the contract, then perfect tender was made, since Bing would have taken the epoxy "as is" and the defect would breach no contractual term. In that case, Bing would not have been entitled to reject the goods; it would not recover any of the damages noted below; and it would be liable to Super for rejecting the goods and will need to pay the full contract price.)

Cover / consequential damages

Bing is likely able to recover that part of the increased price of epoxy reflecting a higher market price (if any), but will have a harder time recovering the increased price of epoxy reflecting quick delivery.

In general, where a seller breaches by delivering non-conforming goods, a buyer is entitled to seek cover by procuring the same goods on the market, and recover the difference between the cover price and the contract price. Thus, to the extent Bing's cover price is higher because the same goods now cost more on the market, it is able to get that difference from Super.

However, consequential damages (damages particular to a particular non breaching party) are generally not recoverable unless the breaching party could reasonably foresee such damages at the time of contract. Here, to the extent Bing's cover price is higher because it needed the goods faster, such difference would instead be consequential damages. Bing would have to show that Super could foresee that Bing would have incurred these costs to avoid a shutdown of its production line. It would probably be difficult for Bing to show with sufficient certainty what level of damages would have been foreseeable to Super at the time the contract was made on February 1. Thus, Bing will have a harder time getting that portion of damages from Super.

Incidental damages

Loss due to the 50 defective surfboards is incidental damages which Bing may recover from Super.

When a contract is breached, the non-breaching party may always recover incidental damages, which are damages relating directly to the handling of the nonconforming goods. Since Super has breached and Bing has incurred incidental damages relating to the defective surfboards, it can get damages for that from Super.

Super's suit against Bing

The analyses regarding governing law, contract formation, terms of the contract and perfect tender are all the same as above.

Rejecting cure

Super likely will not prevail on the point of Bing rejecting the replacement shipment.

Under the UCC and the perfect tender rule, once the time for performance has passed, seller is not entitled to cure by shipping conforming goods unless it knows it is reasonable for it to do so at that time. Here, the time for performance had passed by six days by the time Super told Bing it was shipping replacement epoxy, during which time Bing had already told Super about the issue and that Bing was returning the defective epoxy. As an industrial merchant, Super should probably be familiar with the manufacturing processes of its clients and should probably be aware that there is at least a good probability that a six day delay is too long for a manufacturing customer, which would probably have made cover arrangements during that period. Thus, Super probably can't show that it was reasonable to provide conforming goods six days late.

In short, Super will fail on this claim.

Not paying

Super likely will also fail on its claim to get Bing to pay under the contract.

Once perfect tender is not made, the buyer is entitled to reject the goods, cease performance and not pay. Here, Bing has properly rejected the goods, and it is therefore entitled to not pay.

If Bing had, instead, kept the defective epoxy, Super would probably be able to recover under a restitutionary theory for Bing's enrichment (in that case, though, Super's recovery would have been based on the value of the defective epoxy, not the contract price). But since Bing rejected, it was not enriched, and Super would not be able to recover under that theory either.

In short, Super will fail on this claim as well.

QUESTION 6: SELECTED ANSWER B

Governing Law

All contracts except for contracts for the sale of goods are governed by the common law. Contracts for the sale of goods are governed by Article 2 of the UCC. Article 2 of the UCC provides special rules for contracts between merchants. Here, the contract was for the sale of a movable good, epoxy. A merchant is an entity that regularly deals in goods of the kind in question. Here, Bing regularly ordered epoxy as part of its manufacturing and Super regularly sold epoxy. Therefore, both parties were merchants and the special rules for merchants applied.

Formation of Contract

Offer and Acceptance

To be valid a contract must contain an offer and acceptance as well as mutual assent. An offer is an expression of intent to enter into a contract, communicated to the offeree, as by making a promise, undertaking, or commitment. The terms of the offer must be sufficiently definite to enable a court to enforce the resulting contract. For a contract for the sale of goods, an offer must indicate the subject matter of the contract and contain a quantity term. An offer is accepted by an expression of assent to the terms of the offer communicated to the offeror.

Here, Bing made a valid offer to Super, indicating the subject matter, epoxy, and the quantity, 400 gallons. Further, Bing indicated an intent to enter into a contract. Super's acknowledgment, however, did not constitute an acceptance. Under the UCC, the "battle of the forms" provision controls the terms of a contract when the terms of the acceptance vary from the offer. Here, Super's acceptance contained additional terms to the contract. Ordinarily, additional terms to the contract will become a part of the contract, unless 1) the terms materially modify the contract, 2) the offer expressly limits acceptance to its terms, or 3) the offeror has objected or objects to the additional terms within a reasonable time. If an acceptance indicates that it is conditional on assent to additional terms, it is not construed as an acceptance, but as a rejection and a counteroffer. Therefore, Super's acknowledgment was not an acceptance of Bing's offer, but rather a rejection and counteroffer. Because Bing did not accept the counteroffer, a contract could only be formed by conduct.

Additionally, even if the acknowledgment had not been conditional on assent to additional terms, the additional terms would likely not have become part of the contract. This is because the terms were material alterations of the contract. A term is considered to be material where it alters or in some way limits the available remedies. Here, the additional terms disclaimed warranties of fitness and merchantability, and disclaimed liability for consequential damages. This would severely limit the remedies available to Bing in the event of breach. Because these were material alterations, they would not become part of the contract under the UCC.

Consideration

To be valid, a contract must have consideration, which is a bargained-for legal detriment by both parties or a consideration substitute. A legal detriment may consist of promises exchanged for each other. Here, if a contract was formed between the parties, there would be consideration. Super promised to provide 400 gallons of epoxy. If Bing accepted the contract by conduct, it would become obligated to pay the stated purchase price. Therefore there was an exchange of promises. Alternatively, if the offer and acknowledgment formed no contract, a consideration substitute might be found through promissory estoppel. Promissory estoppel results when a party makes a promise, intending to induce the reliance of the other party, and the other party foreseeably relies on that promise to its detriment.

<u>Bing's Suit Against Super</u>

Breach of Contract

The first issue is whether Super breached its contract with Bing. Because Super's acknowledgment form constituted a counteroffer, which was not accepted by Bing, a contract could only have been formed by conduct. A court would find an implied in fact contract from the shipment of the goods and payment for the goods. However, the terms of Super's acknowledgment would not become part of the contract unless accepted by Bing, which they were not. As a result, Super's disclaimer of warranty and consequential damages was ineffective. Because the disclaimers were ineffective, Super's goods would include an implied warranty of merchantability. The implied warranty of merchantability provides that when a seller of a particular type of goods sells that good, that the goods will be commercially reasonable and will be fit for the ordinary purpose for which such goods are used. Here, Super's epoxy failed to harden properly because of a manufacturing defect. As a result, Super breached the implied warranty of merchantability.

Under the UCC, shipments of goods are governed by the perfect tender rule. Under the perfect tender rule, goods must completely conform to the buyer's specifications or they may be rejected. Any deviation from the buyer's specifications or from commercial suitability is a material breach allowing the buyer to reject the goods. A breach of the implied warranty of merchantability would be a material breach of contract under the perfect tender rule entitling the buyer to reject the shipment. Because the epoxy did not harden properly and was defective, Bing was entitled to reject the shipment. Further, there would be no contract until Bing paid for the goods. Because Bing did not pay for the goods, there was no enforceable contract except to the extent one was created by conduct or promissory estoppel. Super's shipment of epoxy would then be construed as an offer which could be rejected at Bing's discretion.

Super may have also breached the implied warranty of fitness for a particular purpose. The implied warranty of fitness provides that when a seller of goods knows of the particular purpose for which the buyer is using the goods, and the buyer is relying on the seller's skill and judgment in selecting the goods, that the goods must be fit for the particular purpose for which they are used. If Bing had informed Super that it was using the epoxy to make surfboards, and was relying on Super's skill and judgment to furnish epoxy which would be suitable for the purpose, then Super would breach this contract when the epoxy was not suitable for use in making surfboards.

Rejection

The next issue is whether Bing properly rejected the shipment of epoxy. A buyer has a right to inspect the goods before acceptance. Therefore, it was appropriate for Bing to test the epoxy before determining whether to accept the shipment. A buyer of goods may reject a shipment of goods by notifying the seller within a reasonable time of the defect and of intention to reject the goods and returning them. The buyer may accept all the units, or accept some commercial units and reject the rest. Here, Bing tested the epoxy and notified Super a little over a week after the shipment. This would probably constitute a reasonable time after receiving the shipment. Bing returned the defective goods to Super. Therefore, Bing's rejection of the shipment was proper.

Implied in Law or Implied in Fact Contract

A court might find that there was no contract because Bing rejected the offer created by Super's shipment of the goods and never paid for them. A court might also find that a contract existed on the basis of promissory estoppel. Here, Bing notified Super of its requirements and requested shipment by February 20. Super confirmed that it would ship the goods by February 20. Super was aware and would be deemed to know that Bing was using the epoxy in its manufacturing process and might suffer lost profits if the epoxy was defective. Bing relied on this promise to its detriment by not procuring alternative goods in sufficient time to avoid paying a premium and to avoid shutting down its production line. Therefore, a court could likely find that a contract was implied in law by Bing's justifiable reliance on Super's promise to ship the goods by February 20.

On the basis of an implied in law contract, Bing could likely prevail in its suit against Super because it justifiably relied to its detriment on Super's representation that it would ship the epoxy by February 20. If, however, a court found that there was no contract, Bing would not be able to recover any contractual damages.

Damages

Bing would be able to recover compensatory expectation damages from Super for the breach if there was indeed a contract. Expectation damages are designed to put the nonbreaching party in the position it would have been in had the other party properly performed. In a contract for the sale of goods, where the buyer is forced to cover, the buyer must make a good faith effort to obtain a reasonable replacement within a reasonable time. The buyer can recover the difference between the cover price and the contract price. Here, Bing could recover the difference between the price it agreed to with Super and the cover price.

Bing might also be able to recover consequential damages in the form of lost profits, as well as incidental damages. To be recoverable, consequential damages must be certain, foreseeable, and unavoidable. Consequential damages are damages over and above expectation damages resulting from special circumstances of which the seller knows at the time of the contract formation. Here, Super was aware that Bing was using the epoxy in its manufacturing process, and could foresee that Bing might suffer lost profits if the epoxy was defective. Super was aware of Bing's special circumstances. Therefore, it would have been foreseeable to Super that Bing might lose money if the epoxy shipment was defective. Moreover, a supplier is deemed to know of a manufacturer's requirements if it knows that the manufacturer is using the goods as part of the manufacturing process. Here, consequential damages would be measured by the costs expended in manufacturing the 50 defective surfboards, and lost profits resulting from the inability to sell those surfboards, if Bing could sell as many surfboards as it could produce and was a lost volume seller. This would be a sufficiently certain measure of damages because it would be measured by the quantity and cost of defective surfboards produced, as well as any additional surfboards that might have been sold but for the breach. Moreover, Bing made every effort to mitigate its damages and avoid the loss to the extent possible by covering immediately at a reasonable price and reasonable time. Bing might also have incidental damages in locating an alternative supplier of epoxy. Therefore Bing could probably obtain lost profits and incidental damages.

Super's Lawsuit Against Bing

Rejection of Replacement Shipment

Ordinarily when a seller breaches a contract by providing nonconforming goods, the seller has within the time for performance of the contract to cure the breach. Here, Super can argue that because Bing was delayed in notifying Super of the breach, it was not notified within a reasonable time and therefore could not cure within the time for performance. However, likely a court would find that Super was notified within a reasonable time. Because the time for performance of the contract had lapsed, Super had no right to cure the defective shipment. Ordinarily if the seller had reason to believe that the goods would be acceptable with a reasonable allowance, a reasonable additional time might be allowed for the seller to cure. But this is not the case here. Additionally, the fact that Seller was unaware of the manufacturing defects would not grant it additional time to cure. Therefore, Seller had no right to cure.

Paying Under Contract

Because any contract between Bing and Super would be implied rather than actual, Bing would not be liable for payment for the goods if it rejected the goods. Even in a contract formed by mutual assent the buyer would have a right to reject. Further, Super's disclaimers of warranty would not be effective because Super's counteroffer was not accepted. Super's disclaimer might be found to be unconscionable as a contract of adhesion even if it were deemed to have been accepted by Bing. A buyer is deemed to accept those units of the good that he or she actually uses. Further, in an implied in fact contract, there is a contract only to the extent of the goods actually accepted. Therefore, Bing would only be liable for those gallons of epoxy that it used in testing to manufacture the 50 surfboards. Bing would be deemed to accept that quantity of epoxy and would have to pay for it. Otherwise, Bing would not be liable under the contract.

Super is unlikely to prevail in its suit against Bing because there was no mutual assent to terms of a contract. The contract would be implied in law or implied in fact. Further, Super could not disclaim its implied warranty of merchantability in an implied contract. Therefore, Buyer had the right to reject nonconforming shipments, and Super did not cure within the time for performance. Therefore, Bing will not be liable to Super.